365 BIBLE PROMISES *for Busy People*

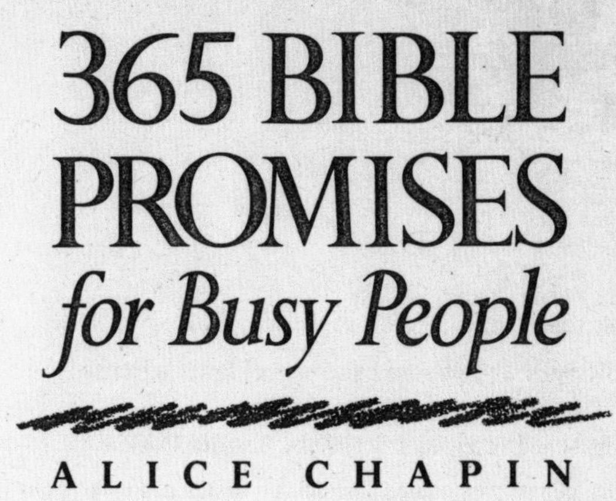

365 BIBLE PROMISES *for Busy People*

ALICE CHAPIN

Living Books®
Tyndale House Publishers, Inc.
Wheaton, Illinois

Library of Congress Card Catalog Number 92-64321
ISBN 0-8423-7048-x

Printed in the United States of America

98 97 96 95 94 93
8 7 6 5

CONTENTS

One

WHY WORRY?

☐ 1 ______________________________

Do not worry about your life, what you will eat; nor about the body, what you will put on. . . . Consider the ravens, for they neither sow nor reap, which have neither storehouse nor barn; and God feeds them. Of how much more value are you than the birds? And which of you by worrying can add one cubit to his stature? (Luke 12:22-25, NKJV).

➢ *Takeaway* **Which of you by worrying can add one cubit to his stature?**

☐ 2 ______________________________

Fear not, for I am with you; be not dismayed, for I am your God. I will strengthen you, yes, I will help you, I will uphold you with My righteous right hand. . . . Fear not, I will help you (Isaiah 41:10, 13, NKJV).

➢ *Takeaway* **Fear not, I will help you.**

☐ 3 ______________________________

Shall I look to the mountain gods for help? No! My help is from Jehovah who made the mountains! And the heavens too! He will never let me stumble, slip, or fall. For he is always watching, never sleeping. Jehovah himself is caring for you! He is your defender. He protects you day and night (Psalm 121:1-6).

➢ *Takeaway* **He is always watching, never sleeping. He protects you day and night.**

☐ 4 ______________________________

Be anxious for nothing, but in everything by prayer and supplication, with thanksgiving, let your requests be made known to God; and the peace of God, which surpasses all understanding, will guard your hearts and minds through Christ Jesus (Philippians 4:6-7, NKJV).

➢ *Takeaway* **Be anxious for nothing.**

☐ 5 ______________________________

He Himself has said, "I will never leave you nor forsake you." So we may boldly say: "The LORD is my helper; I will not fear. What can man do to me?" (Hebrews 13:5-6, NKJV).

➢ *Takeaway* **The Lord is my helper. I will not fear.**

☐ 6 ______________________________

When you pass through the waters, I will be with you; and through the rivers, they shall not overflow you. . . . Fear not, for I am with you. . . . Thus says the Lord, who makes a way in the sea and a path through the mighty waters (Isaiah 43:2, 5, 16, NKJV).

➢ *Takeaway* **Fear not, for I am with you.**

☐ 7 ______________________________

The peace of God, which surpasses all understanding, will guard your hearts and minds through Christ Jesus. . . . Whatever things are true, whatever things are noble, whatever things are just, whatever things are pure, whatever things are lovely, whatever things are of good report, if there is any virtue and if there is anything praiseworthy—meditate on these things (Philippians 4:7-8, NKJV).

➢ *Takeaway* **Whatever things are lovely . . . meditate on these things.**

POWERTHOUGHT It might be a good exercise of soul for us to analyze our thoughts for a few days, and see how many thoughts we actually do give to God's comforts compared with the number we give to our own discomforts.

—H. W. Smith

Two

WHEN YOU FEEL UNLOVED

☐ 8 ______________________________

May your roots go down deep into the soil of God's marvelous love; and may you be able to feel and understand, as all God's children should, how long, how wide, how deep, and how high his love really is; and to experience this love for yourselves, though it is so great that you will never see the end of it or fully know or understand it. And so at last you will be filled up with God himself (Ephesians 3:17-19).

➢ *Takeaway* **May your roots go down deep into the soil of God's marvelous love.**

☐ 9 ______

All praise to him who always loves us and who set us free from our sins by pouring out his lifeblood for us. . . . Because of what Christ has done, we have become gifts to God that he delights in, for as part of God's sovereign plan we were chosen from the beginning to be his (Revelation 1:5; Ephesians 1:11).

➢ *Takeaway* **We have become gifts to God that he delights in.**

☐ 10 ______

When my bones were being formed, carefully put together in my mother's womb, when I was growing there in secret, you knew that I was there—you saw me before I was born. The days allotted to me had all been recorded in your book (Psalm 139:15-16, TEV).

➢ *Takeaway* **When my bones were being formed, carefully put together in my mother's womb, you knew that I was there.**

☐ 11 ______

Hide your loved ones in the shelter of your presence, safe beneath your hand, safe from all conspiring men. Blessed is the Lord, for he has shown me that his never-failing love protects me like the walls of a fort (Psalm 31:20-21).

➢ *Takeaway* **His never-failing love protects me like the walls of a fort.**

☐ 12 ______________________________

I have created you and cared for you since you were born. I will be your God through all your lifetime, yes, even when your hair is white with age. I made you and I will care for you. I will carry you along and be your Savior. . . . The very hairs of your head are all numbered (Isaiah 46:3-4; Matthew 10:30).

➢ *Takeaway* **I made you and I will be your God through all your lifetime.**

☐ 13 ______________________________

The Father himself loves you dearly because you love me and believe that I came from the Father. . . . The Lord says, "I will make my people strong with power from me! They will go wherever they wish, and wherever they go they will be under my personal care" (John 16:27; Zechariah 10:12).

➢ *Takeaway* **My people will go wherever they wish, and wherever they go, they will be under my personal care.**

☐ 14 ______________________________

We know how much God loves us because we have felt his love and because we believe him when he tells us that he loves us dearly. . . . We need have no fear of someone who loves us perfectly; his perfect love for us eliminates all dread of what he might do to us. If we are afraid, it is for fear of what he might do to us and shows that we are not fully convinced that he really loves us (1 John 4:16, 18).

➢ *Takeaway* **His perfect love for us eliminates all dread of what he might do to us.**

POWERTHOUGHT There is no moment when his eye is off me, or his attention is distracted from me, no moment therefore, when his care falters. I never go unnoticed. Every moment of life is spent in the sight and company of an omniscient, omnipresent Creator.

—J. I. Packer, *Knowing God*

Three

WHEN YOU FEEL WEAK, INCAPABLE

☐ 15

Three different times I begged God to make me well again. Each time he said, "No. But I am with you; that is all you need. My power shows up best in weak people." Now I am glad to boast about how weak I am; I am glad to be a living demonstration of Christ's power, instead of showing off my own power and abilities. . . . When I am weak, then I am strong—the less I have, the more I depend on him (2 Corinthians 12:8-10).

➢ *Takeaway* **When I am weak, then I am strong. The less I have, the more I depend on him.**

☐ 16 ________________________________

Even when we are too weak to have any faith left, he remains faithful to us and will help us, for he cannot disown us who are part of himself, and he will always carry out his promises to us. . . . I can do everything God asks me to with the help of Christ who gives me the strength and power (2 Timothy 2:13; Philippians 4:13).

➢ *Takeaway* **I can do everything God asks me to with the help of Christ who gives me the strength and power.**

☐ 17 ________________________________

Christ is not weak in his dealings with you but is a mighty power within you. His weak, human body died on the cross, but now he lives by the mighty power of God. We, too, are weak in our bodies, as he was, but now we live and are strong, as he is, and have all of God's power to use. . . . Strong is your arm! Strong is your hand! Your right hand is lifted high in glorious strength (2 Corinthians 13:3-4; Psalm 89:13).

➢ *Takeaway* **Christ is a mighty power within you. We have all of God's power to use.**

☐ 18 ________________________________

In your strength I can scale any wall, attack any troop. . . . He fills me with strength and protects me wherever I go. He gives me the surefootedness of a mountain goat upon the crags. He leads me safely along the top of the cliffs (Psalm 18:29, 32-33).

➢ *Takeaway* **He fills me with strength and protects me wherever I go.**

☐ 19 ______________________________

I pray that you will begin to understand how incredibly great his power is to help those who believe him. It is that same mighty power that raised Christ from the dead and seated him in the place of honor at God's right hand in heaven (Ephesians 1:19-20).

➢ *Takeaway* **God's power to help those who believe him is that same mighty power that raised Christ from the dead.**

☐ 20 ______________________________

By your power I can crush an army; by your strength I leap over a wall. . . . He causes the good to walk a steady tread like mountain goats upon the rocks. . . . You have made wide steps for my feet, to keep them from slipping. . . . No wonder I give thanks to you, O Lord. . . . God can do what men can't! (2 Samuel 22:30, 34-37, 50; Luke 18:27).

➢ *Takeaway* **God can do what men can't!**

☐ 21

The Lord God is my strength; he will give me the speed of a deer and bring me safely over the mountains. . . . We never give up. Though our bodies are dying, our inner strength in the Lord is growing every day (Habakkuk 3:19; 2 Corinthians 4:16).

➢ *Takeaway* **The Lord God is my strength.**

POWERTHOUGHT Christianity is not just some nice little thing. The gospel of Christ is power. Power to change you. Power to change me. Power to give us victory. Power to keep us going. Power to make creative thinkers of us. Power to help us do a successful job in life. It is power. That is why all those people went for him on that Palm Sunday long ago.

—Norman Vincent Peale

Four

WHEN YOU FEEL DISSATISFIED

☐ 22 ______________________________

Rich man! Proud man! Wise man! You must die like all the rest! You have no greater lease on life than foolish, stupid men. You must leave your wealth to others. . . . They cannot take it with them. . . . Lord, grant us peace; for all we have and are has come from you (Psalm 49:10, 14; Isaiah 26:12).

➢ *Takeaway* **Lord, grant us peace, for all we have and are has come from you.**

☐ 23 ________________________________

The more lowly your service to others, the greater you are. To be the greatest, be a servant. But those who think themselves great shall be disappointed and humbled; and those who humble themselves shall be exalted (Matthew 23:11-12).

➢ *Takeaway* **The more lowly your service to others, the greater you are.**

☐ 24 ________________________________

There is great gain in godliness combined with contentment; for we brought nothing into the world, so that we can take nothing out of it. . . . The love of money is a root of all kinds of evil, and in their eagerness to be rich some have wandered away from the faith and pierced themselves with many pains. But as for you, man of God, shun all this; pursue righteousness, godliness, faith, love, endurance, gentleness (1 Timothy 6:6-7, 10-11, NRSV).

➢ *Takeaway* **There is great gain in godliness with contentment.**

☐ 25 ________________________________

They are to do good, to be rich in good works, generous, and ready to share, thus storing up for themselves the treasure of a good foundation for the future, so that they may take hold of life that really is life (1 Timothy 6:18-19, NRSV).

➢ *Takeaway* **Be liberal and generous so you may take hold of the life that is life indeed.**

☐ 26 ______________________________

Long ago, even before he made the world, God chose us to be his very own. . . . God's purpose in this was that we should praise God and give glory to him for doing these mighty things for us. . . . All you . . . who . . . trusted Christ, were marked as belonging to Christ by the Holy Spirit (Ephesians 1:4, 12-13).

➢ *Takeaway* **God's purpose was that we should praise God and give glory to him.**

☐ 27 ______________________________

A Christian who doesn't amount to much in this world should be glad, for he is great in the Lord's sight (James 1:9).

➢ *Takeaway* **A Christian who doesn't amount to much in this world should be glad, for he is great in the Lord's sight.**

☐ 28 ______________________________

All who humble themselves before the Lord shall be given every blessing and shall have wonderful peace. . . . It is better to have little and be godly than to own an evil man's wealth. . . .The Lord takes care of those he has forgiven. . . . Keep traveling steadily along his pathway and in due season he will honor you with every blessing (Psalm 37:11, 16-17, 34).

➢ *Takeaway* **All who humble themselves before the Lord shall be given every blessing and shall have wonderful peace.**

POWERTHOUGHT There are two ways of being rich. One is to have all you want, the other is to be satisfied with what you have.

Five

WHEN YOU FEEL LIKE COMPLAINING

☐ 29 ________________________________

He has showered down upon us the richness of his grace—for how well he understands us and knows what is best for us at all times (Ephesians 1:8).

➢ *Takeaway* **How well he understands us and knows what is best for us at all times.**

☐ 30 ________________________________

I said to myself, I'm going to quit complaining! I'll keep quiet, especially when the ungodly are around me. But as I stood there silently the turmoil within me grew to the bursting point. The more I mused, the hotter the fires inside. Then at last I spoke and pled with God: Lord, help me to realize how brief my time on earth will be. Help me to know that I am here for but a moment more. . . . Lord, I am speechless before you. I will not open my mouth to speak one word of complaint (Psalm 39:1-4, 9).

➢ *Takeaway* **Lord, help me to realize how brief my time on earth will be.**

☐ 31 ______________________________

Since we have such a huge crowd of men of faith watching us from the grandstands, let us strip off anything that slows us down or holds us back, and especially those sins that wrap themselves so tightly around our feet and trip us up; and let us run with patience the particular race that God has set before us. Keep your eyes on Jesus, our leader and instructor. . . . Think about his patience as sinful men did such terrible things to him. After all, you have never yet struggled against sin and temptation until you sweat great drops of blood (Hebrews 12:1-4).

➢ *Takeaway* **Let us run with patience the particular race that God has set before us.**

☐ 32 ______________________________

In everything you do, stay away from complaining and arguing, so that no one can speak a word of blame against you. You are to live clean, innocent lives as children of God in a dark world full of people who are crooked and stubborn. Shine out among them like beacon lights (Philippians 2:14-15).

➢ *Takeaway* **In everything you do, stay away from complaining and arguing.**

☐ 33 ______________________________

Stay away from the love of money; be satisfied with what you have. . . . Wherever there is jealousy or selfish ambition, there will be disorder and every other kind of evil (Hebrews 13:5; James 3:16).

➢ *Takeaway* **Wherever there is jealousy or selfish ambition, there will be disorder and every other kind of evil.**

☐ 34 ______________________________

I have learned how to get along happily whether I have much or little. I know how to live on almost nothing or with everything. I have learned the secret of contentment in every situation, whether it be a full stomach or hunger, plenty or want; for I can do everything God asks me to with the help of Christ who gives me the strength and power. . . . I came naked from my mother's womb and I shall have nothing when I die. The Lord gave me everything and they are his to take away (Philippians 4:11-13; Job 1:21).

➢ *Takeaway* **The Lord gave me everything and they are his to take away.**

☐ 35 ______________________________

Don't criticize and speak evil about each other, dear brothers. If you do, you will be fighting against God's law of loving one another, declaring it is wrong. But your job is not to decide whether this law is right or wrong, but to obey it. Only he who made the law can rightly judge among us. . . . So what right do you have to judge or criticize others? (James 4:11-12).

➢ *Takeaway* **What right do you have to judge or criticize others?**

POWERTHOUGHT Neglect a personal grievance for forty-eight hours, and it will very likely die.

Six

WHEN YOU FEEL IMPATIENT

☐ 36

Dear brothers who are waiting for the Lord's return, be patient, like a farmer who waits until the autumn for his precious harvest to ripen. . . . Job is an example of a man who continued to trust the Lord in sorrow; from his experiences we can see how the Lord's plan finally ended in good, for he is full of tenderness and mercy (James 5:7, 11).

➢ *Takeaway* **From [Job's] experiences we can see how the Lord's plan finally ended in good, for he is full of tenderness and mercy.**

☐ 37 ______________________________

When the Holy Spirit controls our lives he will produce this kind of fruit in us: love, joy, peace, patience, kindness, goodness, faithfulness, gentleness and self-control. . . . May the Lord bring you into an ever deeper understanding of the love of God and of the patience that comes from Christ (Galatians 5:22; 2 Thessalonians 3:5).

➢ *Takeaway* **When the Holy Spirit controls our lives he will produce . . . patience.**

☐ 38 ______________________________

Is your life full of difficulties and temptations? Then be happy, for when the way is rough, your patience has a chance to grow. So let it grow, and don't try to squirm out of your problems. For when your patience is finally in full bloom, then you will be ready for anything, strong in character, full and complete (James 1:2-4).

➢ *Takeaway* **When the way is rough, your patience has a chance to grow. So let it grow.**

☐ 39 ______________________________

Open the gates to everyone, for all may enter in who love the Lord. He will keep in perfect peace all those who trust in him, whose thoughts turn often to the Lord! (Isaiah 26:2-3).

➢ *Takeaway* **He will keep in perfect peace all those who trust in him, whose thoughts turn often to the Lord!**

☐ 40 ________________________________

We can rejoice, too, when we run into problems and trials, for we know that they are good for us—they help us learn to be patient. And patience develops strength of character in us and helps us trust God more each time we use it until finally our hope and faith are strong and steady. Then, when that happens, we are able to hold our heads high no matter what happens and know that all is well, for we know how dearly God loves us (Romans 5:3-5).

➢ *Takeaway* **We can rejoice when we run into problems and trials for we know that they help us learn to be patient.**

☐ 41 ________________________________

Trust in the Lord. . . . Be delighted with the Lord. . . . Rest in the Lord; wait patiently for him to act. . . . Don't fret and worry—it only leads to harm. . . . But all who humble themselves before the Lord shall be given every blessing and shall have wonderful peace (Psalm 37:3-4, 7-8, 11).

➢ *Takeaway* **Rest in the Lord; wait patiently for him to act. Don't fret and worry—it only leads to harm.**

☐ 42

May God who gives patience, steadiness, and encouragement help you to live in complete harmony with each other—each with the attitude of Christ toward the other. And then all of us can praise the Lord together with one voice, giving glory to God, the Father of our Lord Jesus Christ (Romans 15:5-6).

➢ *Takeaway* **May God who gives patience, steadiness, and encouragement help you to live in complete harmony with each other.**

POWER THOUGHT Be patient, O be patient! Put your ear against the earth;

Listen there how noiselessly the germ o' the seed has birth;

How noiselessly and gently it up heaves its little way

Till it parts the scarcely broken ground, and the blade stands up in day.

—William James Linton

BONUS POWER THOUGHT The race is not always to the swift; there is more to life than increasing its speed.

—William James Linton

Seven

WHEN YOU FEEL BORED WITH LIFE

☐ 43 ______________________________

The backslider gets bored with himself; the godly man's life is exciting. . . . Jesus explained: "My nourishment comes from doing the will of God who sent me" (Proverbs 14:14; John 4:34).

➢ *Takeaway* **The godly man's life is exciting.**

☐ 44 ______________________________

For everything there is a season, and a time for every matter under heaven: a time to be born, and a time to die; a time to plant, and a time to pluck up what is planted. . . . a time to weep, and a time to laugh; a time to mourn, and a time to dance. . . . He has made everything suitable for its time (Ecclesiastes 3:1-2, 4, 11, NRSV).

➢ *Takeaway* **He has made everything suitable for its time.**

☐ 45 ______________________________

We are anxious that you keep right on loving others as long as life lasts, so that you will get your full reward. Then, knowing what lies ahead for you, you won't become bored with being a Christian nor become spiritually dull and indifferent (Hebrews 6:11-12).

➢ *Takeaway* **Keep right on loving others as long as life lasts; then you won't become bored with being a Christian nor spiritually dull or indifferent.**

☐ 46 ______________________________

As for me, my contentment is not in wealth but in seeing you and knowing all is well between us. And when I awake in heaven, I will be fully satisfied, for I will see you face to face (Psalm 17:15).

➢ *Takeaway* **Lord, my contentment is in knowing all is well between us.**

☐ 47 ______________________________

The Lord himself is my inheritance, my prize. He is my food and drink, my highest joy! . . . Heart, body, and soul are filled with joy. . . . You have let me experience the joys of life and the exquisite pleasures of your own eternal presence (Psalm 16:5, 9, 11).

➢ *Takeaway* **The Lord himself is my inheritance, my prize, my highest joy!**

☐ 48 ______________________________

Only good men enjoy life to the full (Proverbs 2:21).

➢ *Takeaway* **Only good men enjoy life to the full.**

☐ 49 ______________________________

Apart from him who can eat or who can have enjoyment? For to the one who pleases him God gives wisdom and knowledge and joy; but to the sinner he gives the work of gathering and heaping, only to give to one who pleases God. This also is vanity and a chasing after wind (Ecclesiastes 2:25-26, NRSV).

➢ *Takeaway* **To the one who pleases him, God gives wisdom and knowledge and joy.**

POWER THOUGHT Boredom is the desire for desires.

—Leo Tolstoy

Eight

WHEN YOU FEEL DISCOURAGED

☐ 50

O God, . . . come quickly! Help! . . . I will keep on expecting you to help me. I praise you more and more. I cannot count the times when you have faithfully rescued me. . . . Your power and goodness, Lord, reach to the highest heavens. . . . Where is there another God like you? You have let me sink down deep in desperate problems. But you will bring me back to life again, up from the depths. . . . You will give me greater honor than before and turn again and comfort me (Psalm 71:12, 14-15, 19-21).

➢ *Takeaway* **I cannot count the times when you have faithfully rescued me.**

☐ 51 ______________________________

Lord, you are my refuge! Don't let me down! Save me from my enemies, for you are just! Rescue me! Bend down your ear and listen to my plea and save me. . . . Hallelujah! Thank you, LORD! How good you are! Your love for us continues on forever. Who can ever list the glorious miracles of God? Who can ever praise him half enough? . . . Blessed be the Lord, the God of Israel, from everlasting to everlasting. Let all the people say, "Amen!" Hallelujah! (Psalms 71:1-2; 106:1-2, 48).

➢ *Takeaway* **Lord, you are my refuge.**

☐ 52 ______________________________

Take a new grip with your tired hands, stand firm on your shaky legs, and mark out a straight, smooth path for your feet so that those who follow you, though weak and lame, will not fall and hurt themselves, but become strong. . . . This is the secret: *Christ in your hearts is your only hope of glory.* . . . I can do it only because Christ's mighty energy is at work within me (Hebrews 12:12-13; Colossians 1:27, 29).

➢ *Takeaway* **Christ's mighty energy is at work within me.**

☐ 53 ______

I am troubled, I am bowed down greatly; I go mourning all the day long. . . . I am feeble and severely broken; I groan because of the turmoil of my heart. Lord, all my desire is before You; and my sighing is not hidden from You. My heart pants, my strength fails me; as for the light of my eyes, it also has gone from me. . . . In You, O LORD, I hope; You will hear, O Lord my God. . . . O my God, be not far from me! . . . These things I have spoken to you, that in Me you may have peace. In the world you will have tribulation; but be of good cheer, I have overcome the world (Psalm 38:6, 8-10, 15, 21; John 16:33, NKJV).

➢ *Takeaway* **Be of good cheer, I have overcome the world.**

☐ 54 ______

Lord, with all my heart I thank you. I will sing your praises before the armies of angels. . . . Your promises are backed by all the honor of your name. When I pray, you answer me and encourage me by giving me the strength I need. . . . The Lord will work out his plans for my life—for your loving-kindness, Lord, continues forever (Psalm 138:1-3, 8).

➢ *Takeaway* **The Lord will work out his plans for my life.**

☐ 55 ______________________________

You are the God of my strength. . . . Oh, send out Your light and Your truth! Let them lead me. . . . Why are you cast down, O my soul? And why are you disquieted within me? Hope in God; for I shall yet praise Him, the help of my countenance and my God (Psalm 43:2-3, 5, NKJV).

➢ *Takeaway* **Hope in God.**

☐ 56 ______________________________

Bless the Lord who is my immovable Rock. . . . Bend down the heavens, Lord, and come. The mountains smoke beneath your touch. Let loose your lightning bolts, your arrows, Lord. . . . Reach down from heaven and rescue me; deliver me from deep waters. . . . I will sing you a new song, O God, with a ten-stringed harp. For you grant victory. . . . Let not your heart be troubled. You are trusting God, now trust in me (Psalm 144:1, 5-7, 9-10; John 14:1).

➢ *Takeaway* **Bless the Lord who is my immovable Rock.**

POWERTHOUGHT The winter is past, the rain is over and gone. The flowers are springing up and the time of the singing of birds has come.

(Song of Solomon 2:11-12).

Nine

WHEN YOU FEEL RESENTFUL

☐ 57 ______________________________

Rid yourselves of all malice and all deceit, hypocrisy, envy, and slander of every kind. Like newborn babies, crave pure spiritual milk, so that by it you may grow up in your salvation (1 Peter 2:1-2, NIV).

➢ *Takeaway* **Grow up in your salvation.**

☐ 58 ______________________________

Make every effort to live in peace with all men and to be holy; without holiness no one will see the Lord. See to it that no one misses the grace of God and that no bitter root grows up to cause trouble and defile (Hebrews 12:14-15, NIV).

➢ *Takeaway* **See to it that no bitter root grows up to cause trouble and defile.**

☐ 59 ____________________________________

The lamp of the LORD searches the spirit of a man; it searches out his inmost being (Proverbs 20:27, NIV).

➢ *Takeaway* **The lamp of the Lord searches out man's inmost being.**

☐ 60 ____________________________________

Do to others as you would have them do to you. . . . Be merciful, just as your Father is merciful. . . . Give, and it will be given to you. . . . For with the measure you use, it will be measured to you (Luke 6:31, 36, 38, NIV).

➢ *Takeaway* **Be merciful, just as your Father is merciful.**

☐ 61 ____________________________________

Fools start fights everywhere while wise men try to keep peace. There's no use arguing with a fool. He only rages and scoffs, and tempers flare. . . . Do you want justice? . . . Ask the Lord for it! (Proverbs 29:8-9, 26).

➢ *Takeaway* **Do you want justice? Ask the Lord for it!**

☐ 62 ______

Remind the people . . . to be ready to do whatever is good, to slander no one, to be peaceable and considerate, and to show true humility toward all men (Titus 3:1-2, NIV).

➢ *Takeaway* **Slander no one.**

☐ 63 ______

Be patient with everyone. Make sure that nobody pays back wrong for wrong, but always try to be kind to each other (1 Thessalonians 5:14-15, NIV).

➢ *Takeaway* **Make sure nobody pays back wrong for wrong.**

POWERTHOUGHT Indignation is the seducer of thought. No man can think clearly when his fists are clenched.

Ten

WHEN YOU FEEL THANKFUL

☐ 64

Give thanks to the Lord of lords, for his loving-kindness continues forever. Praise him who alone does mighty miracles, for his loving-kindness continues forever. Praise him who made the heavens, for his loving-kindness continues forever (Psalm 136:3-5).

➢ *Takeaway* **His loving-kindness continues forever.**

☐ 65

I will sing praise to my God while I have my being. My meditation of him shall be sweet: I will be glad in the LORD. . . . Bless thou the LORD, O my soul. Praise ye the LORD. O give thanks unto the LORD; call upon his name: make known his deeds among the people. Sing unto him, sing psalms unto him: talk ye of all his wondrous works. Glory ye in his holy name: let the heart of them rejoice that seek the LORD. Seek the LORD, and his strength: seek his face evermore. Remember his marvelous works that he hath done; his wonders. . . . He is the LORD our God (Psalms 104:33-35; 105:1-5, 7, KJV).

➢ *Takeaway* **Glory ye in his holy name. He is the LORD our God.**

☐ 66 ________________________________

It is a good thing to give thanks unto the LORD, and to sing praises unto thy name, O most High: To show forth thy lovingkindness in the morning, and thy faithfulness every night, upon an instrument of ten strings, and upon the psaltery; upon the harp with a solemn sound. . . . O LORD, how great are thy works! and thy thoughts are very deep (Psalm 92:1-3, 5, KJV).

➢ *Takeaway* **O LORD, how great are thy works!**

☐ 67 ________________________________

Let the saints be joyful in glory; let them sing aloud. . . . Let the high praises of God be in their mouth. . . . Praise ye the LORD. . . . Praise him for his mighty acts: praise him according to his excellent greatness. Praise him with the sound of the trumpet: praise him with the psaltery and harp. . . . Praise him upon the loud cymbals: praise him upon the high sounding cymbals. Let every thing that hath breath praise the LORD. Praise ye the LORD (Psalms 149:5-6; 150:1-3, 5-6, KJV).

➢ *Takeaway* **Let the saints be joyful.**

☐ 68 ______________________________

Let the redeemed of the LORD say so. . . . Oh that men would praise the LORD for his goodness, and for his wonderful works to the children of men! For he satisfieth the longing soul, and filleth the hungry soul with goodness (Psalm 107:2, 8-9, KJV).

➢ *Takeaway* **Praise the LORD for his goodness, and for his wonderful works to the children of men!**

☐ 69 ______________________________

Among the gods there is none like unto thee, O Lord; neither are there any works like unto thy works. . . . I will praise thee, O Lord my God, with all my heart: and I will glorify thy name forevermore. For great is thy mercy toward me (Psalm 86:8, 12-13, KJV).

➢ *Takeaway* **I will glorify thy name forevermore.**

☐ 70 ______________________________

O give thanks unto the God of gods: for his mercy endureth for ever. . . . To him that by wisdom made the heavens . . . to him that stretched out the earth above the waters . . . to him that made great lights . . . the sun to rule by day . . . the moon and stars to rule by night . . . who giveth food to all flesh. . . . O give thanks unto the God of heaven: for his mercy endureth for ever (Psalm 136:2, 5-9, 25-26, KJV).

➢ *Takeaway* **Give thanks unto the God of gods who made the sun to rule by day, the moon and stars to rule by night.**

POWERTHOUGHT The man who was praying said, "We thank thee for all these gifts, for our food, for our water . . ." I do not know what else was said in the prayer, but that thought gripped me. Thank God for the water. I have asked the blessing before thousands of meals, but that day for the first time I thanked the Lord in spirit and in truth for common ordinary water and for the Living Water. I then began to think of other common things for which we never thank God and began thanking him.

—Donald Grey Barnhouse

Eleven

WHEN YOU FEEL ALONE, LONELY

☐ 71

You both precede and follow me and place your hand of blessing on my head. This is too glorious, too wonderful to believe! I can *never* be lost to your Spirit! I can *never* get away from my God! If I go up to heaven, you are there: if I go down to the place of the dead, you are there. If I ride the morning winds to the farthest oceans, even there your hand will guide me, your strength will support me (Psalm 139:5-10).

➢ *Takeaway* **You both precede and follow me and place your hand of blessing on my head.**

☐ 72 ________________________________

The Lord your God is with you wherever you go. . . . Who then can ever keep Christ's love from us? When we have trouble or calamity, when we are hunted down or destroyed, is it because he doesn't love us anymore? And if we are hungry or penniless or in danger or threatened with death, has God deserted us? No. . . . Victory is ours through Christ who loved us enough to die for us (Joshua 1:9; Romans 8:35-37).

➢ *Takeaway* **The Lord your God is with you wherever you go.**

☐ 73 ________________________________

You belong to Christ Jesus, and though you once were far away from God, now you have been brought very near to him because of what Jesus Christ has done for you with his blood. . . . Now you are no longer strangers to God and foreigners to heaven, but you are members of God's very own family, citizens of God's country, and you belong in God's household with every other Christian (Ephesians 2:13, 19).

➢ *Takeaway* **You are no longer strangers to God, but you are members of God's very own family.**

☐ 74 ________________________________

I will ask the Father and he will give you another Comforter, and he will never leave you. He is the

Holy Spirit, the Spirit who leads into all truth. . . . No, I will not abandon you or leave you as orphans in the storm—I will come to you (John 14:16-18).

➢ *Takeaway* **The Father will give you another Comforter, and he will never leave you. He is the Holy Spirit.**

☐ 75 ________________________________

He knows about everyone, everywhere. . . . When you go through deep waters and great trouble, I will be with you. When you go through rivers of difficulty, you will not drown! . . . I will instruct you (says the Lord) and guide you along the best pathway for your life; I will advise you and watch your progress. . . . I am with you always, even to the end of the world (Hebrews 4:13; Isaiah 43:2; Psalm 32:8; Matthew 28:20).

➢ *Takeaway* **I am with you always, even to the end of the world.**

☐ 76 ________________________________

We live within the shadow of the Almighty, sheltered by the God who is above all gods. This I declare, that he alone is my refuge, my place of safety; he is my God, and I am trusting him (Psalm 91:1-2).

➢ *Takeaway* **We live within the shadow of the Almighty, sheltered by the God who is above all gods.**

☐ 77

The Lord . . . is close to all who call on him sincerely. He fulfills the desires of those who reverence and trust him; he hears their cries for help and rescues them. He protects all those who love him. . . . If my father and mother should abandon me, you would welcome and comfort me (Psalms 145:17-20; 27:10).

➢ *Takeaway* **The Lord is close to all who call on him sincerely.**

POWERTHOUGHT When I walk by the wayside, He is along with me. When I enter into company amid all my forgetfulness of Him, He never forgets me. In the silent watches of the night, when my eyelids are closed and my spirit has sunk into unconsciousness, the observant eye of Him who never slumbers is upon me. I cannot flee from His presence. Go where I will, He leads me, and watches me, and cares for me. The same Being who is now at work in the remotest domains of nature and of providence is also at my hand to make more full every moment of my being.
—Chalmers (a nineteenth-century Scottish churchman)

Twelve

WHEN YOU FEEL SICK IN BODY OR SPIRIT

☐ 78 ________________________________

Hear my prayer, O Lord; listen to my cry! Don't sit back, unmindful of my tears. For I am your guest. I am a traveler passing through the earth, as all my fathers were. Spare me, Lord! Let me recover and be filled with happiness again. . . . Is anyone among you suffering? He should keep on praying about it. . . . The earnest prayer of a righteous man has great power and wonderful results (Psalm 39:12-13; James 5:13-16).

➢ *Takeaway* **The earnest prayer of a righteous man has great power and wonderful results.**

☐ 79 ______________________________

I cried to you for help, O LORD my God, and you healed me; you kept me from the grave. I was on my way to the depths below, but you restored my life. Sing praise to the LORD, all his faithful people! Remember what the Holy One has done. . . . Tears may flow in the night, but joy comes in the morning (Psalm 30:2-5, TEV).

➢ *Takeaway* **Tears may flow in the night, but joy comes in the morning.**

☐ 80 ______________________________

When Jesus had come down from the hill with the apostles, he stood on a level place with a large number of his disciples. A large crowd of people was there. . . . They had come to hear him and to be healed of their diseases. . . . All the people tried to touch him, for power was going out from him and healing them all. . . . Jesus Christ is the same yesterday, today, and forever (Luke 6:17-19; Hebrews 13:8, TEV).

➢ *Takeaway* **Jesus Christ is the same yesterday, today, and forever.**

☐ 81 ______________________________

How weary we grow of our present bodies. That is why we look forward eagerly to the day when we shall have heavenly bodies that we shall put on like new clothes (2 Corinthians 5:2).

➢ *Takeaway* **We look forward eagerly to the day when we shall have heavenly bodies.**

☐ 82 ______________________________

We are often troubled, but not crushed; sometimes in doubt, but never in despair; there are many enemies, but we are never without a friend. . . . We never become discouraged. Even though our physical being is gradually decaying, yet our spiritual being is renewed day after day (2 Corinthians 4:8-9, 16, TEV).

➢ *Takeaway* **We are never without a friend.**

☐ 83 ______________________________

He listens to me every time I call to him. The danger of death was all around me; the horrors of the grave closed in on me; I was filled with fear and anxiety. . . . The Lord protects the helpless; when I was in danger, he saved me. Be confident, my heart, because the LORD has been good to me (Psalm 116:2-3, 6-7, TEV).

➢ *Takeaway* **Be confident my heart.**

☐ 84 ______________________________

I was given a painful physical ailment. . . . Three times I prayed to the Lord about this and asked him to take it away. But his answer was: "My grace is all you need, for my power is greatest when you are weak." I am most happy, then, to be proud of my weaknesses, in order to feel the protection Christ's power over me. I am content with weaknesses, insults, hardships, persecutions, and difficulties for Christ's sake. For when I am weak, then I am strong (2 Corinthians 12:7-10, TEV).

➢ *Takeaway* **My grace is all you need, for my power is greatest when you are weak.**

POWERTHOUGHT Many men owe the grandeur of their lives to their tremendous difficulties.

Thirteen

WHEN YOU FEEL AFRAID

☐ 85

Hear my cry, O God; attend to my prayer. From the end of the earth I will cry to You, when my heart is overwhelmed; lead me to the rock that is higher than I. . . . He only is my rock and my salvation; He is my defense; I shall not be greatly moved (Psalms 61:1-2; 62:2, NKJV).

➢ *Takeaway* **He is my rock and my salvation.**

☐ 86

I will pray morning, noon, and night, pleading aloud with God; and he will hear and answer. Though the tide of battle runs strongly against me, for so many are fighting me, yet he will rescue me. . . . O God, have pity, for I am trusting you! I will hide beneath the shadow of your wings until this storm is past (Psalms 55:17-18; 57:1).

➢ *Takeaway* **I will hide beneath the shadow of your wings until this storm is past.**

☐ 87 ______________________________

Because you have made the LORD, who is my refuge, even the Most High, your dwelling place, no evil shall befall you, nor shall any plague come near your dwelling; for He shall give His angels charge over you, to keep you in all your ways. In their hands they shall bear you up, lest you dash your foot against a stone (Psalm 91:9-12, NKJV).

➢ *Takeaway* **He shall give His angels charge over you, to keep you in all your ways.**

☐ 88 ______________________________

Is not God your Father? Has he not created you? . . . God protected them [Israel] in the howling wilderness as though they were the apple of his eye. He spreads his wings over them, even as an eagle overspreads her young. She carries them upon her wings—as does the Lord his people! . . . Even when walking through the dark valley of death I will not be afraid, for you are close beside me, guarding, guiding all the way. . . . Your goodness and unfailing kindness shall be with me all of my life (Deuteronomy 32:6, 10-11; Psalm 23:4, 6).

➢ *Takeaway* **You are close beside me, guarding, guiding all the way.**

☐ 89 ____________________

The eyes of the Lord are watching over those who fear him, who rely upon his steady love. . . . We depend upon the Lord alone to save us. Only he can help us; he protects us like a shield. . . . Yes, Lord, let your constant love surround us, for our hopes are in you alone (Psalm 33:18-20, 22).

➢ *Takeaway* **He protects us like a shield.**

☐ 90 ____________________

The Lord is my fort where I can enter and be safe; no one can follow me in and slay me. He is a rugged mountain where I hide; he is my Savior, a rock where none can reach me, and a tower of safety. He is my shield. He is like the strong horn of a mighty fighting bull (Psalm 18:2).

➢ *Takeaway* **The Lord is my fort where I can enter and be safe.**

☐ 91 ____________________

Don't be anxious about tomorrow. God will take care of your tomorrow too. Live one day at a time. . . . Since the Lord is directing our steps, why try to understand everything that happens along the way? (Matthew 6:34; Proverbs 20:24).

➢ *Takeaway* **Live one day at a time.**

POWERTHOUGHT

Be still, my soul: thy best, thy heav'nly Friend,
Thro' thorny ways leads to a joyful end.

—From the hymn "Be Still My Soul"

Fourteen

WHEN YOU FEEL HURT, HUMILIATED

☐ 92 ______________________________

He upholds the cause of the oppressed and gives food to the hungry. The LORD sets prisoners free, the LORD gives sight to the blind, the LORD lifts up those who are bowed down, the LORD loves the righteous. The LORD watches over the alien and sustains the fatherless and the widow. . . . The LORD reigns forever (Psalm 146:7-10, NIV).

➢ *Takeaway* **The LORD upholds the cause of the oppressed.**

☐ 93 ___

The LORD . . . heals the brokenhearted and binds up their wounds. . . . Great is our Lord and mighty in power; his understanding has no limit. . . . The LORD delights in those who fear him, who put their hope in his unfailing love (Psalm 147:2-3, 5, 11, NIV).

➢ *Takeaway* **The LORD heals the brokenhearted and binds up their wounds.**

☐ 94 ___

The Lord is close to those whose hearts are breaking; he rescues those who are humbly sorry for their sins. The good man does not escape all troubles—he has them too. But the Lord helps him in each and every one (Psalm 34:18-19).

➢ *Takeaway* **The Lord is close to those whose hearts are breaking.**

☐ 95 ___

The LORD is compassionate and gracious, slow to anger, abounding in love. . . . As a father has compassion on his children, so the LORD has compassion on those who fear him; for he knows how we are formed, he remembers that we are dust (Psalm 103:8, 13-14, NIV).

➢ *Takeaway* **The Lord is compassionate.**

☐ 96 ___

The time will come when God's redeemed will all come home again. . . . Sorrow and mourning will all disappear. I, even I, am he who comforts you and give you all this joy (Isaiah 51:11-12).

➢ *Takeaway* **God's redeemed will all come home again. Sorrow and mourning will all disappear.**

☐ 97 ___

In God's eyes he was like a tender green shoot, sprouting from a root in dry and sterile ground. But in our eyes there was no attractiveness at all, nothing to make us want him. . . . But he was wounded and bruised for our sins. He was beaten that we might have peace; he was lashed—and we were healed! . . . He was oppressed and he was afflicted, yet he never said a word. He was brought as a lamb to the slaughter; and as a sheep before her shearers is dumb, so he stood silent before the ones condemning him (Isaiah 53:2, 5, 7).

➢ *Takeaway* **In God's eyes he was like a tender green shoot, sprouting from a root in dry and sterile ground.**

☐ 98 ___

Even when we are too weak to have any faith left, he remains faithful to us and will help us, for he cannot disown us who are part of himself, and he will always carry out his promises to us (2 Timothy 2:13).

➢ *Takeaway* **Even when we are too weak to have any faith left, he remains faithful to us and will help us.**

POWERTHOUGHT Only the wounded can serve.

Fifteen

WHEN GUILT COMES

☐ 99

There is not a righteous man on earth who *continually* does good and who never sins. . . . Search me, O God, and know my heart; try me and know my anxious thoughts; and see if there be any hurtful way in me, and lead me in the everlasting way (Ecclesiastes 7:20; Psalm 139:23-24, NASB).

➢ *Takeaway* **Search me, O God, and know my heart. See if there be any hurtful way in me.**

☐ 100 ______________________________

In this man Jesus there is forgiveness for your sins! Everyone who trusts in him is freed from all guilt and declared righteous (Acts 13:38-39).

➢ *Takeaway* **Everyone who trusts in him is freed from all guilt and declared righteous.**

☐ 101 ______________________________

There was a time when I wouldn't admit what a sinner I was. But my dishonesty made me miserable and filled my days with frustration. All day and all night your hand was heavy on me. My strength evaporated like water on a sunny day until I finally admitted all my sins to you. . . . And you forgave me! All my guilt is gone (Psalm 32:3-5).

➢ *Takeaway* **I admitted all my sins to you, Lord. All my guilt is gone.**

☐ 102 ______________________________

We are saved by faith in Christ and not by the good things we do. . . . Let us come boldly to the very throne of God and stay there to receive his mercy and to find grace to help us in our times of need (Romans 3:28; Hebrews 4:16).

➢ *Takeaway* **Let us come boldly to the very throne of God to receive his mercy and to find grace.**

☐ 103 ________________

Bless the Lord, O my soul; and all that is within me, bless His holy name . . . who pardons all your iniquities. . . . For as high as the heavens are above the earth, so great is His lovingkindness toward those who fear Him. As far as the east is from the west, so far has He removed our transgressions from us (Psalm 103:1, 3, 11-12, NASB).

➢ *Takeaway* **As far as the east is from the west, so far has He removed our transgressions from us.**

☐ 104 ________________

Long ago, even before he made the world, God chose us to be his very own through what Christ would do for us; he decided then to make us holy in his eyes, without a single fault—we who stand before him covered with his love. . . . We have become gifts to God that he delights in (Ephesians 1:4, 11).

➢ *Takeaway* **We stand before him covered with his love, without a single fault.**

☐ 105 ________________

"Come now, and let us reason together," says the LORD. "Though your sins are as scarlet, they will be as white as snow; though they are red like crimson, they will be like wool." . . . Truly, the mouth of the LORD has spoken (Isaiah 1:18, 20, NASB).

➢ *Takeaway* **Though your sins are as scarlet, they will be as white as snow.**

POWERTHOUGHT All man's troubles come from not knowing how to sit still in one room.

—Pascal, *Pensées*, 1670

Sixteen

WHEN YOU ARE TEMPTED

☐ 106

After this manner therefore pray ye: Our Father which art in heaven. . . . Lead us not into temptation, but deliver us from evil (Matthew 6:9, 13, KJV).

➢ *Takeaway* **Pray ye: deliver us from evil.**

☐ 107

Let no one say when he is tempted, "I am being tempted by God"; for God cannot be tempted by evil, and He Himself does not tempt anyone. But each one is tempted when he is carried away and enticed by his own lust. Then when lust has conceived, it gives birth to sin (James 1:13-15, NASB).

➢ *Takeaway* **God does not tempt anyone.**

☐ 108 ______________________________

You are my hiding place from every storm of life; you even keep me from getting into trouble! You surround me with songs of victory (Psalm 32:7).

➢ *Takeaway* **You are my hiding place.**

☐ 109 ______________________________

Happy are those whose hearts are pure, for they shall see God (Matthew 5:8).

➢ *Takeaway* **Happy are those whose hearts are pure.**

☐ 110 ______________________________

What do you think the Scripture means when it says that the Holy Spirit, whom God has placed within us, watches over us with tender jealousy? But he gives us more and more strength to stand against . . . evil longings (James 4:5-6).

➢ *Takeaway* **The Holy Spirit gives us strength to stand against evil longings.**

☐ 111 ______________________________

Your strength must come from the Lord's mighty power within you. Put on all of God's armor so that you will be able to stand safe against all strategies and tricks of Satan. . . . You will need the strong belt of truth and the breastplate of God's approval. . . . In every battle you will need faith as your shield. . . . And you will need the helmet of salvation and the sword of the Spirit—which is the Word of God. Pray all the time (Ephesians 6:10-11, 14, 16-18).

➢ *Takeaway* **Put on all of God's armor so you will be able to stand safe against all strategies and tricks of Satan.**

☐ 112 ___

Lord, who may go and find refuge and shelter in your tabernacle up on your holy hill? Anyone who leads a blameless life and is truly sincere. Anyone who refuses to slander others, does not listen to gossip, never harms his neighbor, speaks out against sin, criticizes those committing it, commends the faithful followers of the Lord, keeps a promise even if it ruins him, does not crush his debtors with high interest rates, and refuses to testify against the innocent despite the bribes offered him—such a man shall stand firm forever (Psalm 15).

➢ *Takeaway* **Lord, who may find refuge on your holy hill? Anyone who leads a blameless life.**

POWERTHOUGHT Integrity is a lot easier when you remember that someone else is in the room with you at all times.

Seventeen

WHEN YOU ARE TOO BUSY

☐ 113

There is a right time for everything: a time to be born; a time to die; a time to plant; a time to harvest . . . a time to cry; a time to laugh . . . a time to hug; a time not to hug . . . a time to be quiet; a time to speak up; a time for loving; a time for hating; a time for war; a time for peace. . . . Everything is appropriate in its own time (Ecclesiastes 3:1-8, 11).

➢ *Takeaway* **There is a right time for everything. Everything is appropriate in its own time.**

☐ 114 ______

My life is no longer than my hand! My whole lifetime is but a moment to you. Proud man! Frail as breath! A shadow! And all his busy rushing ends in nothing. He heaps up riches for someone else to spend. And so, Lord, my only hope is in you. . . . For I am your guest. I am a traveler passing through the earth, as all my fathers were. . . . "Come unto me and I will give you rest—all of you that work so hard beneath a heavy yoke. Wear my yoke—for it fits perfectly. . . for I give you only light burdens (Psalm 39:5-7, 12; Matthew 11:28-30).

➢ *Takeaway* **Come unto me and I will give you rest.**

☐ 115 ______

Before the mountains were brought forth, or ever thou hadst formed the earth and the world, even from everlasting to everlasting, thou art God. . . . A thousand years in thy sight are but as yesterday when it is past, and as a watch in the night. . . . So teach us to number our days, that we may apply our hearts to wisdom. . . . Establish thou the work of our hands (Psalm 90:2, 4, 12, 17, KJV).

➢ *Takeaway* **A thousand years in thy sight are but as yesterday when it is past, and as a watch in the night.**

☐ 116

He that loveth silver shall not be satisfied with silver; nor he that loveth abundance with increase: this is also vanity. When goods increase . . . what good is there to the owners thereof, saving the beholding of them with their eyes? . . . As he came forth of his mother's womb, naked shall he return to go as he came, and shall take nothing of his labour. . . . Follow me. For whosoever will save his life shall lose it: and whosoever will lose his life for my sake shall find it. For what is a man profited, if he shall gain the whole world, and lose his own soul? (Ecclesiastes 5:10-11, 15; Matthew 16:24-26, KJV).

➢ *Takeaway* **What is a man profited, if he shall gain the whole world, and lose his own soul?**

☐ 117

The peace of God, which passeth all understanding, shall keep your hearts and minds through Christ Jesus. . . . Whatsoever things are true, whatsoever things are honest, whatsoever things are just, whatsoever things are pure, whatsoever things are lovely, whatsoever things are of good report; if there be any virtue, and if there be any praise, think on these things. . . . I can do all things through Christ which strengtheneth me (Philippians 4:7-8, 13, KJV).

➢ *Takeaway* **I can do all things through Christ which strengtheneth me.**

☐ 118 ______________________________

There shall be a time of anguish . . . greater than any previous suffering. . . . It will not be understood until the end times, when travel and education shall be vastly increased! . . . When you follow your own wrong inclinations . . . there will be wrong doctrine, envy, murder, drunkenness, wild parties and all that sort of thing. . . . Let us follow the Holy Spirit's leading in every part of our lives. Then we won't need to look for honors and popularity, which lead to jealousy and hard feelings (Daniel 12:1, 4; Galatians 5:19-21, 25-26).

➢ *Takeaway* **Let us follow the Holy Spirit's leading in every part of our lives. Then we won't need to look for honors and popularity.**

☐ 119 ______________________________

Many that are first shall be last; and the last first. . . . Whosoever will be great among you, shall be your minister: and whosoever of you will be the chiefest, shall be servant of all. For even the Son of man came not to be ministered unto, but to minister. . . . If ye love me, keep my commandments. . . . Peace I leave with you, my peace I give unto you: not as the world giveth, give I unto you.

Let not your heart be troubled (Mark 10:31, 43-45; John 14:15, 27, KJV).

➢ *Takeaway* **Many that are first shall be last; and the last first.**

POWER THOUGHT On a deathbed, no one ever laments, "I wish I had spent more time at the office."

Eighteen

WHEN YOU DON'T LIKE YOURSELF VERY WELL OR YOU FEEL LIKE A NOBODY

☐ 120

The Lord said to Samuel, "Don't judge by a man's face or height, for this is not the one. I don't make decisions the way you do! Men judge by outward appearance, but I look at a man's thoughts and intentions" (1 Samuel 16:7).

➢ *Takeaway* **Men judge by outward appearance, but God looks at a man's thoughts and intentions.**

☐ 121 ___

You are set apart for God; and he has accepted you because of what the Lord Jesus Christ and the Spirit of our God have done for you. . . . As far as God is concerned there is a sweet, wholesome fragrance in our lives. It is the fragrance of Christ within us, an aroma to both the saved and the unsaved all around us (1 Corinthians 6:11; 2 Corinthians 2:15).

➢ *Takeaway* **As far as God is concerned there is a sweet, wholesome fragrance in our lives.**

☐ 122 ___

God has bought you with a great price. . . . Anyone who believes and says that Jesus is the Son of God has God living in him. . . . I want you to realize that God has been made rich because we who are Christ's have been given to him! (1 Corinthians 6:20; 1 John 4:15; Ephesians 1:18).

➢ *Takeaway* **God has been made rich because we who are Christ's have been given to him!**

☐ 123 ___

Just as there are many parts to our bodies, so it is with Christ's body. We are all parts of it, and it takes every one of us to make it complete, for we each have different work to do. So we belong to each other, and each needs all the others. God has given each of us the ability to do certain things well (Romans 12:4-6).

➢ *Takeaway* **God has given each of us the ability to do certain things well.**

☐ 124 ____________________

Woe to the man who fights with his Creator. Does the pot argue with its maker? Does the clay dispute with him who forms it, saying, "Stop, you're doing it wrong!" or the pot exclaim, "How clumsy can you be!"? Woe to the baby just being born who squalls to his father and mother, "Why have you produced me? Can't you do anything right at all?" Jehovah . . . says: What right have you to question what I do? Who are you to command me concerning the work of my hands? . . . God who began the good work within you will keep right on helping you grow in his grace until his task within you is finally finished on that day when Jesus Christ returns (Isaiah 45:9-11; Philippians 1:6).

➢ *Takeaway* **Woe to the man who fights with his Creator. Does the clay dispute with him who forms it, saying, "Stop, you're doing it wrong"?**

☐ 125 ____________________

God said, "Let us make a man—someone like ourselves, to be the master of all life upon the earth and in the skies and in the seas." So God made man like his Maker. Like God did God make man; man and maid did he make them. . . . Then God looked over all that he had made, and it was excellent in every way (Genesis 1:26-27, 31).

➢ *Takeaway* **Man and maid did God make them, excellent in every way.**

☐ 126

Dear brothers whom God has set apart for himself. . . . You are the world's seasoning, to make it tolerable. If you lose your flavor, what will happen to the world? . . . You are the world's light (Hebrews 3:1; Matthew 5:13-14).

➢ *Takeaway* **You are the world's seasoning whom God has set apart for himself.**

POWER THOUGHT We have missed the full impact of the gospel if we have not discovered what it is to be ourselves loved by God, irreplaceable in his sight, unique among our fellowmen.

—Bruce Larson

BONUS POWER THOUGHTS Of all our infirmities, the most savage is to despise our being.

—Montaigne

There are no ordinary people. You have never talked to a "mere mortal."

—C. S. Lewis

Nineteen

WHEN YOU ARE HAPPY

☐ 127

Is anyone among you . . . happy? He should sing praises (James 5:13, TEV).

➢ *Takeaway* **Happy? Sing praises!**

☐ 128

Praise him, sun and moon; praise him, shining stars. . . . Praise him, kings and all peoples, princes and all other rulers; girls and young men, old people and children too. . . . His name is greater than all others; his glory is above earth and heaven. . . . Praise the LORD! (Psalm 148:3, 11-14, TEV).

➢ *Takeaway* **Praise the LORD!**

☐ 129 ______________________________

Wake up, my soul! Wake up, my harp and lyre! I will wake up the sun. I will thank you, O LORD . . . I will praise you. . . . Your constant love reaches above the heavens; your faithfulness touches the skies (Psalm 108:1-4, TEV).

➢ *Takeaway* **Wake up, my soul! Lord, I will praise you.**

☐ 130 ______________________________

This is the day which the LORD hath made; we will rejoice and be glad in it. . . . Thou art my God, I will exalt thee. . . . With trumpets and sound of cornets make a joyful noise before the LORD, the King. Let the sea roar, and the fulness thereof. . . . Let the floods clap their hands: let the hills be joyful together (Psalms 118:24, 28; 98:6-8, KJV).

➢ *Takeaway* **This is the day which the LORD hath made. Rejoice!**

☐ 131 ______________________________

I will praise you, my God and King, and bless your name each day and forever. . . . I will meditate about your glory, splendor, majesty, and miracles. . . . I will proclaim your greatness (Psalm 145:1-2, 5-6).

➢ *Takeaway* **I will meditate about your glory, splendor, majesty, and miracles.**

☐ 132

O come, let us sing unto the LORD. . . . Let us come before his presence with thanksgiving, and make a joyful noise unto him with psalms. . . . O come, let us worship and bow down: let us kneel before the LORD our maker (Psalm 95:1-2, 6, KJV).

➢ *Takeaway* **Let us come before his presence with thanksgiving.**

☐ 133

Hallelujah! Yes, praise the Lord! . . . Praise him for his mighty works. Praise his unequaled greatness. Praise him with the trumpet and with lute and harp. Praise him with the drums and dancing. Praise him with stringed instruments and horns. Praise him with the cymbals, yes, loud clanging cymbals. Let everything alive give praises to the Lord! *You* praise him! Hallelujah! (Psalm 150).

➢ *Takeaway* **Praise him with cymbals, yes, loud clanging cymbals! Hallelujah!**

POWERTHOUGHT Happiness is not the absence of conflict but the ability to cope with it.

Twenty

HOW TO BE HAPPY

☐ 134 ______

What happiness for those whose guilt has been forgiven! What joys when sins are covered over! What relief for those who have confessed their sins and God has cleared their record (Psalm 32:1-2).

➢ *Takeaway* **What relief for those who have confessed their sins and God has cleared their record.**

☐ 135 ______

Blessed is the man who trusts in the LORD, and whose hope is the LORD. For he shall be like a tree planted by the waters, which spreads out its roots by the river, and will not fear when heat comes; but its leaf will be green, and will not be anxious in the year of drought, nor will cease from yielding fruit (Jeremiah 17:7-8, NKJV).

➢ *Takeaway* **Blessed is the man whose hope is the LORD.**

☐ 136 ______________________________

Happy are those who are humble; they will receive what God has promised! Happy are those whose greatest desire is to do what God requires; God will satisfy them fully! Happy are those who are merciful to others; God will be merciful to them! . . . Happy are those who work for peace; God will call them his children! (Matthew 5:5-7, 9, TEV).

➢ *Takeaway* **Happy are those who are merciful to others.**

☐ 137 ______________________________

If you want a long and satisfying life, closely follow my instructions. Never tire of loyalty and kindness. Hold these virtues tightly. Write them deep within your heart. . . . In everything you do, put God first, and he will direct you and crown your efforts with success (Proverbs 3:2-3, 6).

➢ *Takeaway* **Put God first, and he will direct you and crown your efforts with success.**

☐ 138 ______________________________

If you want a happy, good life, keep control of your tongue, and guard your lips from telling lies. Turn away from evil and do good. Try to live in peace even if you must run after it to catch and hold it! (1 Peter 3:10-11).

➢ *Takeaway* **If you want a happy, good life, keep control of your tongue.**

☐ 139 ______________________________

God has already given you everything you need. . . . He has given you the whole world to use, and life and even death are your servants. He has given you all of the present and all of the future. . . . You belong to Christ, and Christ is God's. . . . *So you have everything when you have Christ* (1 Corinthians 3:21-23; Colossians 2:10).

➢ *Takeaway* **You have everything when you have Christ.**

☐ 140 ______________________________

Follow the steps of the godly . . . and stay on the right path, for only good men enjoy life to the full (Proverbs 2:20-21).

➢ *Takeaway* **Only good men enjoy life to the full.**

POWER THOUGHT Only one life will soon be passed; only what's done for Christ will last.

—Anonymous

Twenty-One

WHEN YOU FEEL BLUE

☐ 141

The Lord lifts the fallen and those bent beneath their loads. . . . He is close to all who call on him sincerely (Psalm 145:14, 18).

➢ *Takeaway* **The Lord lifts those bent beneath their loads.**

☐ 142

All who are oppressed may come to him. He is a refuge for them in their times of trouble. . . . He heals the brokenhearted, binding up their wounds (Psalms 9:9; 147:3).

➢ *Takeaway* **He heals the brokenhearted, binding up their wounds.**

☐ 143 ____________________

Trust the Lord; and remember that other Christians all around the world are going through these sufferings too. After you have suffered a little while, our God, who is full of kindness through Christ, will give you his eternal glory. He personally will come and pick you up, and set you firmly in place, and make you stronger than ever (1 Peter 5:9-10).

➢ *Takeaway* **Christians all around the world are going through these sufferings too.**

☐ 144 ____________________

God . . . the Father of our Lord Jesus Christ, the source of every mercy . . . wonderfully comforts and strengthens us in our hardships and trials. And why does he do this? So that when others are troubled, needing our sympathy and encouragement, we can pass on to them this same help and comfort God has given us (2 Corinthians 1:3-4).

➢ *Takeaway* **God wonderfully comforts and strengthens us in our hardships and trials.**

☐ 145 ____________________

Come to me, all you who are weary and burdened, and I will give you rest. Take my yoke upon you and learn from me, for I am gentle and humble in heart, and you will find rest for your souls (Matthew 11:28-29, NIV).

➢ *Takeaway* **Come to me, all you who are weary and burdened, and I will give you rest.**

☐ 146 ______

Just as you trusted Christ to save you, trust him, too, for each day's problems; live in vital union with him. Let your roots grow down into him and draw up nourishment from him (Colossians 2:6-7).

➢ *Takeaway* **Just as you trusted Christ to save you, trust him, too, for each day's problems.**

☐ 147 ______

Fix your thoughts on what is true and good and right. Think about things that are pure and lovely, and dwell on the fine, good things in others. Think about all you can praise God for and be glad about. . . . Think about the loving-kindness of the Lord! (Philippians 4:8; Psalm 107:43).

➢ *Takeaway* **Think about things that are pure and lovely. Think about all you can praise God for and be glad about.**

POWERTHOUGHT Not cloudless days; not rose-strewn ways; not care-free years, devoid of sorrow's tears—but strength to bear your load of human care, and grace to live aright and keep your raiment white, and love to see you through; that is God's pledge to you.

—Anonymous

Twenty-Two

ANTIDOTE FOR THE BLUES

☐ 148

I waited patiently for the LORD; he inclined to me and heard my cry. He drew me up from the desolate pit, out of the miry bog, and set my feet upon a rock, making my steps secure. He put a new song in my mouth, a song of praise. . . . Happy are those who make the LORD their trust (Psalm 40:1-4, NRSV).

➢ *Takeaway* **He drew me up from the miry bog. He put a new song in my mouth, a song of praise.**

☐ 149 ______________________________

Why are you cast down, O my soul, and why are you disquieted within me? . . . I say to God, my rock: "Why have you forgotten me?" . . . But I trust in you, O LORD. . . . My times are in your hand. . . . Let your face shine upon your servant (Psalms 42:5, 9; 31:14-16, NRSV).

➢ *Takeaway* **My times are in thy hand. Let thy face shine on thy servant.**

☐ 150 ______________________________

O my people in Jerusalem, you shall weep no more, for he will surely be gracious to you at the sound of your cry. He will answer you. Though he give you the bread of adversity and water of affliction, yet he will be with you to teach you—with your own eyes you will see your Teacher (Isaiah 30:19-20).

➢ *Takeaway* **Though he give you the bread of adversity, yet he will be with you to teach you.**

☐ 151 ______________________________

Come, let us return to the Lord; it is he who has torn us—he will heal us. He has wounded—he will bind us up. . . . He will set us on our feet again to live in his kindness! . . . Let us press on to know him, and he will respond to us as surely as the coming of dawn or the rain of early spring (Hosea 6:1-3).

➢ *Takeaway* **He will respond to us as surely as the coming of dawn or the rain of early spring.**

☐ 152 ______________________________

Be patient. . . . Strengthen your hearts. . . . You have heard of the endurance of Job, and you have seen the purpose of the Lord, how the Lord is compassionate and merciful. . . . Are any among you suffering? They should pray. . . . The prayer of the righteous is powerful and effective (James 5:7-8, 11, 13, 16, NRSV).

➢ *Takeaway* **Is any one suffering? Let him pray. The prayer of the righteous is powerful and effective.**

☐ 153 ______________________________

The LORD is a stronghold for the oppressed, a stronghold in times of trouble. And those who know your name put their trust in you, for you, O LORD, have not forsaken those who seek you (Psalm 9:9-10, NRSV).

➢ *Takeaway* **The Lord is a stronghold for the oppressed.**

☐ 154 ______________________________

O my soul, don't be discouraged. Don't be upset. Expect God to act! For I know that I shall again have plenty of reason to praise him for all that he will do. He is my help! He is my God! . . . O my soul, why be so gloomy and discouraged? Trust in God! . . . He will make me smile again (Psalms 42:11; 43:5).

➢ *Takeaway* **O my soul, why be so gloomy and discouraged? He will make me smile again.**

POWER THOUGHT I know the Lord is always with me. He is helping me. God's mighty power supports me (Acts 2:25).

Twenty-Three

DOES GOD HEAR MY CRIES FOR HELP?

☐ 155

The salvation of the righteous is from the LORD; He is their strength in the time of trouble. And the LORD shall help them and deliver them; He shall deliver them from the wicked, and save them, because they trust in Him (Psalm 37:39-40, NKJV).

➢ *Takeaway* **The salvation of the righteous is from the Lord.**

☐ 156

I waited patiently for the LORD; and He inclined to me, and heard my cry. He also brought me up out of a horrible pit, out of the miry clay, and set my feet upon a rock, and established my steps. He has put a new song in my mouth—praise to our God (Psalm 40:1-3, NKJV).

➢ *Takeaway* **The LORD inclined to me and heard my cry.**

☐ 157 ______________________________

The eyes of the LORD are on the righteous, and His ears are open to their cry. . . . The righteous cry out, and the LORD hears (Psalm 34:15, 17, NKJV).

➢ *Takeaway* **The righteous cry out, and the LORD hears.**

☐ 158 ______________________________

In the LORD I put my trust. . . . The LORD is righteous; He loves righteousness; His countenance beholds the upright (Psalm 11:1, 7, NKJV).

➢ *Takeaway* **His countenance beholds the upright.**

☐ 159 ______________________________

I called on the LORD in distress; the LORD answered me and set me in a broad place. The LORD is on my side; I will not fear. What can man do to me? . . . It is better to trust in the LORD than to put confidence in man (Psalm 118:5-6, 8, NKJV).

➢ *Takeaway* **The LORD is on my side; I will not fear.**

☐ 160 ______________________________

Delight yourself also in the LORD, and He shall give you the desires of your heart. Commit your way to the LORD, trust also in Him, and He shall bring it to pass. . . . Wait on the LORD (Psalm 37:4-5, 34, NKJV).

➢ *Takeaway* **He shall bring it to pass. Wait on the Lord.**

☐ 161 ______________________________

From the end of the earth I will cry to You, when my heart is overwhelmed; lead me to the rock that is higher than I. . . . I will abide in Your tabernacle forever; I will trust in the shelter of Your wings. For You, O God, have heard my vows (Psalm 61:2, 4-5, NKJV).

➢ *Takeaway* **Lead me to the Rock that is higher than I.**

POWERTHOUGHT You and I may take hold at any time upon the justice and the mercy and the faithfulness and the wisdom, the long-suffering and the tenderness of God, and we shall find there every attribute of the Most High to be, as it were, a great battering ram with which we may open the gates of heaven.

—Charles Haddon Spurgeon

Twenty-Four

IS GOD INTERESTED IN ME?

☐ 162 ______________________________

How precious it is, Lord, to realize that you are thinking about me constantly! I can't even count how many times a day your thoughts turn toward me. And when I waken in the morning, you are still thinking of me! . . . God's truth stands firm like a great rock, and nothing can shake it. It is a foundation stone with these words written on it: "The Lord knows those who are really his" (Psalm 139:17-18; 2 Timothy 2:19).

➢ *Takeaway* **How precious it is, Lord, to realize that you are thinking about me constantly!**

☐ 163 ______

Have I not commanded you? Be strong and courageous. Do not be terrified; do not be discouraged, for the LORD your God will be with you wherever you go. . . . Surely God is my help; the Lord is the one who sustains me (Joshua 1:9; Psalm 54:4, NIV).

➢ *Takeaway* **God is my help; the Lord is the one who sustains me.**

☐ 164 ______

Aren't five sparrows sold for two pennies? Yet not one sparrow is forgotten by God. Even the hairs of your head have all been counted. So do not be afraid; you are worth much more than many sparrows! (Luke 12:6-7, TEV).

➢ *Takeaway* **Even the hairs of your head have all been counted.**

☐ 165 ______

Leave all your worries with him, because he cares for you. . . . The LORD keeps close watch over the whole world, to give strength to those whose hearts are loyal to him (1 Peter 5:7; 2 Chronicles 16:9, TEV).

➢ *Takeaway* **The LORD keeps close watch over the whole world, to give strength to those whose hearts are loyal to him.**

☐ 166 ____________________

He holds our lives in his hands, and he holds our feet to the path. . . . I will tell you what he did for me: For I cried to him for help with praises ready on my tongue. . . . He listened! He heard my prayer! He paid attention to it! Blessed be God, who didn't turn away when I was praying, and didn't refuse me his kindness and love (Psalm 66:9, 16-18, 20).

➢ *Takeaway* **I cried to him for help! He listened! He heard my prayer! He paid attention to it!**

☐ 167 ____________________

He has put his brand upon us—his mark of ownership—and given us his Holy Spirit in our hearts as guarantee that we belong to him and as the first installment of all that he is going to give us (2 Corinthians 1:22).

➢ *Takeaway* **He has put his brand upon us.**

☐ 168 ____________________

You know everything I do; from far away you understand all my thoughts. You see me, whether I am working or resting; you know all my actions. Even before I speak, you already know what I will say. You are all around me on every side; you protect me with your power (Psalm 139:2-5, TEV).

➢ *Takeaway* **You see me whether I am working or resting.**

POWER THOUGHT God's love for me is the one constant left in life today. It is the same each day, each hour, forever.

BONUS POWER THOUGHT I know not where his islands lift their fronded palms in air; I only know I cannot drift beyond his love and care.

—John Greenleaf Whittier

Twenty-Five

DOES GOD UNDERSTAND HOW I FEEL?

☐ 169 ______________________________

I am poor and weak, yet the Lord is thinking about me right now! O my God, you are my helper. You are my Savior. . . . You have seen me tossing and turning through the night. You have collected all my tears and preserved them in your bottle! You have recorded every one in your book (Psalms 40:17; 56:8).

➢ *Takeaway* **You have collected all my tears and preserved them in your bottle!**

☐ 170 ______

The LORD upholds all those who fall and lifts up all who are bowed down. . . . The LORD is near to all who call on him (Psalm 145:14, 18, NIV).

➢ *Takeaway* **The Lord upholds all those who fall.**

☐ 171 ______

"Comfort, yes, comfort my people," says your God. . . . Don't you yet understand? Don't you know by now that the everlasting God, the Creator of the farthest parts of the earth, never grows faint or weary? No one can fathom the depths of his understanding. He gives power to the tired and worn out, and strength to the weak (Isaiah 40:1, 28-29).

➢ *Takeaway* **He gives power to the tired and worn out, and strength to the weak.**

☐ 172 ______

Since he himself has now been through suffering and temptation, he knows what it is like when we suffer and are tempted, and he is wonderfully able to help us (Hebrews 2:18).

➢ *Takeaway* **He himself has been through suffering; he knows what it is like when we suffer.**

☐ 173 ____________________

The LORD is close to the brokenhearted. . . . [He] crowns you with love and compassion (Psalms 34:18; 103:4, NIV).

➢ *Takeaway* **The LORD is close to the broken-hearted.**

☐ 174 ____________________

The steadfast love of the LORD never ceases, his mercies never come to an end; they are new every morning; great is your faithfulness. "The LORD is my portion," says my soul, "therefore I will hope in him" (Lamentations 3:22-24, NRSV).

➢ *Takeaway* **His mercies are new every morning.**

☐ 175 ____________________

I will bind you to me forever with chains of righteousness and justice and love and mercy (Hosea 2:19).

➢ *Takeaway* **I will bind you to me forever with chains of love and mercy.**

POWER THOUGHT God is often compassionate to us through the compassion of others.

Twenty-Six

DOES GOD PROTECT HIS OWN?

☐ 176

The Lord says, "I will make my people strong with power from me! They will go wherever they wish, and wherever they go they will be under my personal care" (Zechariah 10:12).

➢ *Takeaway* **Wherever they go, my people will be under my personal care.**

☐ 177

Who will protect me from the wicked? Who will be my shield? I would have died unless the Lord had helped me. I screamed, "I'm slipping, Lord!" and he was kind and saved me. Lord, when doubts fill my mind, when my heart is in turmoil, quiet me and give me renewed hope and cheer (Psalm 94:16-19).

➢ *Takeaway* **Lord, when doubts fill my mind, when my mind is in turmoil, quiet me and give me renewed hope and cheer.**

☐ 178 ________________

The LORD is your keeper; the LORD is your shade at your right hand. The sun shall not strike you by day, nor the moon by night. The LORD shall preserve you from all evil; He shall preserve your soul. The LORD shall preserve your going out and your coming in from this time forth, and even forevermore (Psalm 121:5-8, NKJV).

➢ *Takeaway* **The LORD is your keeper . . . your shade at your right hand.**

☐ 179 ________________

The LORD is my light and my salvation; whom shall I fear? The LORD is the strength of my life; of whom shall I be afraid? . . . Though an army may encamp against me, my heart shall not fear. . . . In the time of trouble He shall hide me in His pavilion; in the secret place of His tabernacle He shall hide me; He shall set me high upon a rock (Psalm 27:1, 3, 5, NKJV).

➢ *Takeaway* **In the time of trouble, he shall hide me in his pavilion. He shall set me high upon a rock.**

☐ 180 ________________________________

The Angel of the Lord guards and rescues all who reverence him. . . . Even strong young lions sometimes go hungry, but those of us who reverence the Lord will never lack any good thing. Sons and daughters, come and listen and let me teach you the importance of trusting and fearing the Lord (Psalm 34:7, 10-11).

➢ *Takeaway* **The Angel of the Lord guards and rescues all who reverence him.**

☐ 181 ________________________________

Whenever I am afraid, I will trust in You. . . . When I cry out to You, then my enemies will turn back. This I know, because God is for me. . . . In God I have put my trust; I will not be afraid. What can man do to me? (Psalm 56:3, 9, 11, NKJV).

➢ *Takeaway* **In God I have put my trust; I will not be afraid.**

☐ 182 ________________________________

The very day I call for help, the tide of battle turns. My enemies flee! This one thing I *know: God is for me!* (Psalm 56:9).

➢ *Takeaway* **This one thing I know: God is for me!**

POWER THOUGHT The light of God surrounds me. The love of God enfolds me. The power of God protects me. The presence of God watches over me. Wherever I am, God is!

—Anonymous

BONUS POWER THOUGHT

A mighty fortress is our God, a bulwark never failing;
Our helper He, amid the flood of mortal ills prevailing.
For still our ancient foe doth seek to work us woe,
His craft and power are great, and armed with cruel hate,
On earth is not his equal.

Did we in our own strength confide, our striving would be losing.
Were not the right Man on our side, the Man of God's own choosing.
Dost ask who that may be? Christ Jesus, it is He;
Lord Sabaoth His name, from age to age the same,
And He must win the battle.

—Martin Luther

Twenty-Seven

WHEN YOUR PROBLEMS SEEM TOO BIG FOR GOD

☐ 183 ______

O LORD my God, you are very great; you are clothed with splendor and majesty. . . . He makes the clouds his chariot and rides on the wings of the wind. . . . He set the earth on its foundations; it can never by moved. You covered it with the deep as with a garment; the waters stood above the mountains. . . . They went down into the valleys, to the place you assigned for them. You set a boundary they cannot cross. . . . Praise the LORD, O my soul (Psalm 104:1, 3, 5-6, 8-9, 35, NIV).

➢ *Takeaway* **O LORD my God, you are very great.**

☐ 184 ______________________________

Not by might, nor by power, but by my Spirit, says the Lord Almighty—you will succeed because of my Spirit, though you are few and weak. . . . I am the Lord, the God of all mankind; is there anything too hard for me? (Zechariah 4:6; Jeremiah 32:27).

➢ *Takeaway* **I am the Lord, the God of all mankind; is there anything too hard for me?**

☐ 185 ______________________________

Now glory be to God, who by his mighty power at work within us is able to do far more than we would ever dare to ask or even dream of—infinitely beyond our highest prayers, desires, thoughts, or hopes (Ephesians 3:20).

➢ *Takeaway* **God is able to do far more than we would ever dare to ask or even dream of.**

☐ 186 ______________________________

Oh, that you would burst forth from the skies and come down! How the mountains would quake in your presence! The consuming fire of your glory would burn down the forests and boil the oceans dry. The nations would tremble before you. . . . For since the world began no one has seen or heard of such a God as ours, who works for those who wait for him! (Isaiah 64:1-2, 4).

➢ *Takeaway* **The consuming fire of your glory would burn down the forests and boil the oceans dry.**

☐ 187 ______________________________

Before the mountains were created, before the earth was formed, you are God without beginning or end. You speak, and man turns back to dust. A thousand years are but as yesterday to you! . . . No mere man has ever seen, heard, or even imagined what wonderful things God has ready for those who love the Lord (Psalm 90:2-4; 1 Corinthians 2:9).

➢ *Takeaway* **Before the mountains were created, before the earth was formed, you are God without beginning or end.**

☐ 188 ______________________________

Because the Lord God helps me, I will not be dismayed; therefore, I have set my face like flint to do his will, and I know that I will triumph. He who gives me justice is near. Who will dare to fight against me now? Where are my enemies? Let them appear! (Isaiah 50:7-8).

➢ *Takeaway* **Because the Lord helps me, I will not be dismayed.**

☐ 189

See, the Lord God is for me! Who shall declare me guilty? All my enemies shall be destroyed like old clothes eaten up by moths (Isaiah 50:9).

➢ *Takeaway* **See, the Lord God is for me!**

POWERTHOUGHT Stop a moment and envision what power it took to blast life back into a dead body and then to lift it up out of a stone cave. Maybe the crisis you are experiencing right now is an opportunity to discover all that God really is.

Twenty-Eight

SEE HOW GOD LOVES ME!

☐ 190 ___

His compassion never ends. . . . Great is his faithfulness; his loving-kindness begins afresh each day. . . . The Lord is wonderfully good to those who wait for him, to those who seek for him (Lamentations 3:22-23, 25).

➢ *Takeaway* **His loving-kindness begins afresh each day.**

☐ 191 ___

The Lord is God! He made us—we are his people, the sheep of his pasture. . . . The Lord is always good. He is always loving and kind, and his faithfulness goes on and on to each succeeding generation (Psalm 100:3, 5).

➢ *Takeaway* **His faithfulness goes on and on to each succeeding generation.**

☐ 192 ____________________

Wherever he [Jesus] went he healed people of every sort of illness. And what pity he felt for the crowds that came, because their problems were so great and they didn't know what to do or where to go for help. They were like sheep without a shepherd. . . . He is our God. We are his sheep, and he is our Shepherd (Matthew 9:35-36; Psalm 95:6).

➢ *Takeaway* **We are his sheep, and he is our Shepherd.**

☐ 193 ____________________

He forgives all my sins. . . . He surrounds me with loving-kindness and tender mercies. He fills my life with good things! . . . He gives justice to all who are treated unfairly. . . . He is merciful and tender toward those who don't deserve it; he is slow to get angry and full of kindness and love. He never bears a grudge, nor remains angry forever. . . . His mercy toward those who fear and honor him is as great as the height of the heavens above the earth (Psalm 103:3-6, 8-9, 11).

➢ *Takeaway* **He surrounds me with loving-kindness and tender mercies. He fills my life with good things!**

☐ 194 ______

You are merciful and gentle, Lord, slow in getting angry, full of constant loving-kindness and of truth. . . . Lord . . . you forgive! What an awesome thing this is! (Psalms 86:15; 130:4).

➢ *Takeaway* **Lord, you forgive! What an awesome thing!**

☐ 195 ______

Your steadfast love, O Lord, is as great as all the heavens. Your faithfulness reaches beyond the clouds. Your justice is as solid as God's mountains. Your decisions are as full of wisdom as the oceans are with water. You are concerned for men and animals alike. . . . You feed them with blessings from your own table and let them drink from your rivers of delight (Psalm 36:5-6, 8).

➢ *Takeaway* **Your faithfulness reaches beyond the clouds.**

☐ 196 ______

Your love and kindness are better to me than life itself. How I praise you! . . . I lie awake at night thinking of you—of how much you have helped me—and how I rejoice through the night beneath the protecting shadow of your wings. I follow close behind you, protected by your strong right arm (Psalm 63:3, 6-8).

➢ *Takeaway* **I rejoice through the night beneath the protecting shadow of your wings.**

POWER THOUGHT The Lord's goodness surrounds us at every moment. I walk through it almost with difficulty, as through thick grass and flowers.

—R. W. Barbour

Twenty-Nine

WHO AM I?

☐ 197

If you believe that Jesus is the Christ—that he is God's Son and your Savior—then you are a child of God (1 John 5:1).

➢ *Takeaway* **You are a child of God.**

☐ 198

All who are led by the Spirit of God are sons of God. And so we should not be like cringing, fearful slaves, but we should behave like God's very own children, adopted into the bosom of his family, and calling to him, "Father, Father" (Romans 8:14-15).

➢ *Takeaway* **We should behave like God's very own children, adopted into the**

bosom of his family, and calling to him, "Father, Father."

☐ 199 ________________

See how very much our heavenly Father loves us, for he allows us to be called his children—think of it—and we really *are!* But since most people don't know God, naturally they don't understand that we are his children. Yes . . . we are already God's children, right now, and we can't even imagine what it is going to be like later on (1 John 3:1-2).

➢ *Takeaway* **We are already God's children, right now!**

☐ 200 ________________

When the right time came . . . he sent his Son . . . to buy freedom for us . . . so that he could adopt us as his very own sons. And because we are his sons, God has sent the Spirit of his Son into our hearts, so now we can rightly speak of God as our dear Father. . . . We are no longer slaves but God's own sons (Galatians 4:4-7).

➢ *Takeaway* **We can rightly speak of God as our dear Father.**

☐ 201 ________________

We who have been made holy by Jesus, now have the same Father he has. That is why Jesus is not ashamed to call us his brothers. For he says in the book of Psalms, "I will talk to my brothers about

God my Father, and together we will sing his praises" (Hebrews 2:11-12).

➢ *Takeaway* **We who have been made holy by Jesus, now have the same Father he has.**

☐ 202 ______________________________

He is not far from any one of us. For in him we live and move and are! As one of your own poets says it, "We are the sons of God" (Acts 17:27-28).

➢ *Takeaway* **In him we live and move and are!**

☐ 203 ______________________________

All honor to God, the God and Father of our Lord Jesus Christ; for it is his boundless mercy that has given us the privilege of being born again so that we are now members of God's own family. . . . Since we are his children, we will share his treasures—for all God gives to his Son Jesus is now ours too (1 Peter 1:3; Romans 8:17).

➢ *Takeaway* **We are now members of God's own family.**

POWERTHOUGHT Imagine God standing in front of you looking into your eyes, then cupping your face in his hands and with adoring eyes, saying to you, "You are my wonderful child. I love you."

BONUS POWER THOUGHT People who know who they are learn to respect themselves and behave themselves better, which is as God probably planned it all along.

Thirty

WHAT DOES GOD WANT OF ME?

☐ 204

What does the LORD require of you but to do justice, and to love kindness, and to walk humbly with your God? (Micah 6:8, NRSV).

➢ *Takeaway* **Do justice, love kindness, walk humbly.**

☐ 205

Anyone wanting to be a leader among you must be your servant. . . . Your attitude must be like my own, for I, the Messiah, did not come to be served, but to serve, and to give my life as a ransom for many (Matthew 20:26, 28).

➢ *Takeaway* **Anyone wanting to be a leader among you must be your servant.**

☐ 206 ______________________________

I don't want your sacrifices—I want your love; I don't want your offerings—I want you to know me (Hosea 6:6).

➢ *Takeaway* **I want your love. I want you to know me.**

☐ 207 ______________________________

Be kindly affectionate to one another with brotherly love, in honor giving preference to one another . . . rejoicing in hope, patient in tribulation, continuing steadfastly in prayer; distributing to the needs of the saints, given to hospitality. . . . Rejoice with those who rejoice, and weep with those who weep. . . . Associate with the humble. Do not be wise in your own opinion. Repay no one evil for evil (Romans 12:10, 12-13, 15-17, NKJV).

➢ *Takeaway* **Be kindly affectionate to one another, patient in tribulation, steadfast in prayer.**

☐ 208 ______________________________

Love one another. . . . Aspire to live quietly, to mind your own affairs, and to work . . . so that you may behave properly toward outsiders and be dependent on no one (1 Thessalonians 4:9, 11-12, NRSV).

➢ *Takeaway* **Love one another.**

☐ 209

Do the good things that result from being saved, obeying God with deep reverence, shrinking back from all that might displease him. . . . You are to live clean, innocent lives as children of God in a dark world full of people who are crooked and stubborn. Shine out among them like beacon lights, holding out to them the Word of Life (Philippians 2:12, 15-16).

➢ *Takeaway* **In a dark world full of people who are crooked and stubborn . . . shine out among them like beacon lights.**

☐ 210

Bear one another's burdens. . . . Let us not grow weary in doing what is right, for we will reap at harvest-time, if we do not give up. . . . Whenever we have an opportunity, let us work for the good of all, and especially for those of the family of faith (Galatians 6:2, 9-10, NRSV).

➢ *Takeaway* **Bear one another's burdens.**

POWER THOUGHT Christ's servants will one day meet and hear from him sweet, sweet words: "Well done."

Thirty-One

WHY AM I HERE ON EARTH?

☐ 211

"Of all the commandments, which is the most important?" Jesus replied, "The one that says, 'Hear, O Israel! The Lord our God is the one and only God. And you must love him with all your heart and soul and mind and strength.' The second is: 'You must love others as much as yourself.' No other commandments are greater than these" (Mark 12:28-31).

➢ *Takeaway* **You must love others as much as yourself.**

☐ 212 ___

All who claim me as their God will come, for I have made them for my glory; I created them. . . . Some . . . people have missed the most important thing in life—they don't know God (Isaiah 43:7; 1 Timothy 6:21).

➢ *Takeaway* **The most important thing in life is to know God.**

☐ 213 ___

I hate your show and pretense—your hypocrisy of "honoring" me with your religious feasts and solemn assemblies. . . . Away with your hymns of praise—they are mere noise to my ears. I will not listen to your music, no matter how lovely it is. I want to see a mighty flood of justice—a torrent of doing good (Amos 5:21, 23-24).

➢ *Takeaway* **I want to see a mighty flood of justice—a torrent of doing good.**

☐ 214 ___

Long ages ago he planned that we should spend these lives in helping others. . . . With Jesus' help we will continually offer our sacrifice of praise to God by telling others of the glory of his name. Don't forget to do good and to share what you have with those in need (Ephesians 2:10; Hebrews 13:15-16).

➢ *Takeaway* **Long ages ago he planned that we should spend these lives in helping others.**

☐ 215

If I had the gift of being able to speak in other languages without learning them and could speak in every language there is in all of heaven and earth, but didn't love others, I would only be making noise. . . . Even if I had the gift of faith so that I could speak to a mountain and make it move, I would still be worth nothing at all without love (1 Corinthians 13:1-2).

➢ *Takeaway* **If I had the gift of faith so that I could speak to a mountain and make it move, I would still be worth nothing at all without love.**

☐ 216

It is God himself, in his mercy, who has given us this wonderful work [of telling his Good News to others], and so we never give up. . . . For God, who said, "Let there be light in the darkness," has made us understand that it is the brightness of his glory that is seen in the face of Jesus Christ (2 Corinthians 4:1, 6).

➢ *Takeaway* **It is God himself who has given us this wonderful work of telling his Good News to others.**

☐ 217 ______

What I want from you is your true thanks; I want your promises fulfilled. *I want you to trust me in your times of trouble, so I can rescue you and you can give me glory* (Psalm 50:14-15).

➢ *Takeaway* **I want you to trust me in your times of trouble so I can rescue you and you can give me glory.**

POWERTHOUGHT Man's chief end is to glorify God and to enjoy him forever.

—Presbyterian Catechism

Thirty-Two

PRAYER CHANGES THINGS

☐ 218

I love the Lord because he hears my prayers and answers them. Because he bends down and listens, I will pray as long as I breathe. . . . Jesus the Son of God is our great High Priest who has gone to heaven itself to help us; therefore let us never stop trusting him. . . . So let us come boldly to the very throne of God and stay there to receive his mercy and to find grace to help us in our times of need (Psalm 116:1-2; Hebrews 4:14, 16).

➢ *Takeaway* **Because he bends down and listens, I will pray as long as I breathe.**

☐ 219 ___

By our faith—the Holy Spirit helps us with our daily problems and in our praying. For we don't even know what we should pray for nor how to pray as we should, but the Holy Spirit prays for us with such feeling that it cannot be expressed in words. And the Father who knows all hearts knows, of course, what the Spirit is saying as he pleads for us in harmony with God's own will (Romans 8:26-27).

➢ *Takeaway* **The Holy Spirit prays for us with such feeling that it cannot be expressed in words.**

☐ 220 ___

When you pray, don't be like the hypocrites who pretend piety by praying publicly on street corners and in the synagogues where everyone can see them. Truly, that is all the reward they will ever get. But when you pray, go away by yourself, all alone, and shut the door behind you and pray to your Father secretly, and your Father, who knows your secrets, will reward you. . . . Remember, your Father knows exactly what you need even before you ask him! (Matthew 6:5-6, 8).

➢ *Takeaway* **When you pray, go away by yourself, all alone, and shut the door behind you and pray to your Father secretly.**

☐ 221 ______________________________

The earnest prayer of a righteous man has great power and wonderful results. . . . The eyes of the Lord are intently watching all who live good lives, and he gives attention when they cry to him. . . . Yes, the Lord hears the good man when he calls to him for help (James 5:16; Psalm 34:15, 17).

➢ *Takeaway* **The earnest prayer of a righteous man has great power and wonderful results.**

☐ 222 ______________________________

When I pray, you answer me and encourage me by giving me the strength I need. . . . Though I am surrounded by troubles, you will bring me safely through them. You will clench your fist against my angry enemies! Your power will save me. . . . O Lord God! You have made the heavens and earth by your great power; nothing is too hard for you! . . . You have all wisdom and do great and mighty miracles (Psalm 138:3, 7; Jeremiah 32:17-19).

➢ *Takeaway* **O Lord God! You have made the heavens and earth by your great power; nothing is too hard for you!**

☐ 223 ______________________________

The Lord . . . delights in the prayers of his people. . . . O God, my God! How I search for you! How I thirst for you in this parched and weary land where there is no water. How I long to find you! How I wish I could go into your sanctuary to see your strength and glory, for your love and kindness are better to me than life itself. How I praise you! I will bless you as long as I live, lifting up my hands to you in prayer. At last I shall be fully satisfied; I will praise you with great joy (Proverbs 15:8; Psalm 63:1-5).

➢ *Takeaway* **The Lord delights in the prayers of his people.**

☐ 224 ______________________

Don't be weary in prayer; keep at it. . . . We are sure of this, that he will listen to us whenever we ask him for anything in line with his will. And if we really know he is listening when we talk to him and make our requests, then we can be sure that he will answer us (Colossians 4:2; 1 John 5:14-15).

➢ *Takeaway* **Don't be weary in prayer; keep at it.**

POWERTHOUGHT You and I may take hold at any time upon the justice and mercy and the faithfulness and the wisdom, the long-suffering and the tenderness of God, and we shall find there every attribute of the Most High to be, as it were, a great battering ram with which we may open the gates of heaven.

—Charles Haddon Spurgeon

BONUS POWER THOUGHT He will listen to the prayers of the destitute, for he is never too busy to heed their requests. . . . The one thing I want from God, the thing I seek most of all, is the privilege of meditating in his Temple, living in his presence every day of my life, delighting in his incomparable perfections and glory (Psalms 102:17; 27:4).

Thirty-Three

BIBLE PRAYERS YOU CAN PRAY

☐ 225 ______________________________

Bless the LORD, O my soul, and all that is within me, bless his holy name. . . . Be exalted, O God, above the heavens, and let your glory be over all the earth (Psalms 103:1; 108:5, NRSV).

➢ *Takeaway* **Be exalted, O God, above the heavens!**

☐ 226 ______________________________

Teach us to count our days that we may gain a wise heart. . . . Satisfy us in the morning with your steadfast love. . . . Let your work be manifest to your servants, and your glorious power to their children. Let the favor of the Lord our God be upon us (Psalm 90:12, 14, 16-17, NRSV).

➢ *Takeaway* **Satisfy us in the morning with your steadfast love.**

☐ 227 ______________________________

O Lord, don't hold back your tender mercies from me! My only hope is in your love and faithfulness. . . . Problems far too big for me to solve are piled higher than my head. Meanwhile my sins, too many to count, have all caught up with me, and I am ashamed to look up. My heart quails within me. Please, Lord, rescue me! Quick! Come and help me! (Psalm 40:11-13).

➢ *Takeaway* **Please, Lord, rescue me! Come and help me!**

☐ 228 ______________________________

May the Lord make you increase and abound in love for one another and for all. . . . May he so strengthen your hearts in holiness that you may be blameless before our God (1 Thessalonians 3:12-13, NRSV).

➢ *Takeaway* **May the Lord make you increase and abound in love.**

☐ 229 ______________________________

As the deer pants for water, so I long for you, O God. . . . Lord, when doubts fill my mind, when my heart is in turmoil, quiet me and give me renewed hope and cheer. . . . The Lord my God is my fortress—the mighty Rock where I can hide (Psalms 42:1; 94:19, 22).

➢ *Takeaway* **When my heart is in turmoil, quiet me.**

☐ 230 ______________________________

I pray that as you share your faith with others it will grip their lives too, as they see the wealth of good things in you that come from Jesus Christ (Philemon 1:6).

➢ *Takeaway* **As you share your faith with others may it grip their lives too.**

☐ 231 ______________________________

Our Father in heaven, hallowed be your name. Your kingdom come, your will be done, on earth as it is in heaven. Give us this day our daily bread. And forgive us our debts, as we also have forgiven our debtors. And do not bring us to the time of trial, but rescue us from the evil one (Matthew 6:9-13, NRSV).

➢ *Takeaway* **Your kingdom come; your will be done.**

POWERTHOUGHT More things are wrought by prayer than this world dreams of.

—Alfred, Lord Tennyson

Thirty-Four

BIBLE PRAYERS FOR MY FAVORITE PERSON

☐ 232

Jesus . . . looked up to heaven and said, . . . "Holy Father, keep them in your own care—all those you have given me. . . . I'm not asking you to take them out of the world, but to keep them safe from Satan's power. . . . Make them pure and holy through teaching them your words of truth" (John 17:1, 11, 15, 17).

➢ *Takeaway* **Make them pure and holy through teaching them your words of truth.**

☐ 233 ______________________________

Let the words of my mouth and the meditation of my heart be acceptable to you, O LORD, my rock and my redeemer (Psalm 19:14, NRSV).

➢ *Takeaway* **Let the words of my mouth and the meditation of my heart be acceptable to you, O Lord.**

☐ 234 ______________________________

Make me to know your ways, O LORD; teach me your paths. Lead me in your truth. . . . . Wondrously show your steadfast love. . . . Guard me as the apple of the eye; hide me in the shadow of your wings (Psalms 25:4-5; 17:7-8, NRSV).

➢ *Takeaway* **Guard me as the apple of the eye.**

☐ 235 ______________________________

This is my prayer: that your love may abound more and more in knowledge and depth of insight, so that you may be able to discern what is best and may be pure and blameless until the day of Christ, filled with the fruit of righteousness that comes through Jesus Christ—to the glory and praise of God (Philippians 1:9-11, NIV).

➢ *Takeaway* **May you be filled with the fruit of righteousness.**

☐ 236 ______

The LORD bless you and keep you; the LORD make his face to shine upon you, and be gracious to you; the LORD lift up his countenance upon you, and give you peace (Numbers 6:24-26, NRSV).

➢ *Takeaway* **The LORD make his face to shine upon you, and be gracious to you.**

☐ 237 ______

This is what I have asked of God for you: . . . that you will have the rich experience of knowing Christ with real certainty and clear understanding. . . . Let your roots grow down into him and draw up nourishment from him. See that you go on growing in the Lord, and become strong and vigorous in the truth you were taught. Let your lives overflow with joy and thanksgiving for all he has done (Colossians 2:2, 7).

➢ *Takeaway* **May you have the rich experience of knowing Christ with real certainty and clear understanding.**

☐ 238 ______

May the Lord make you to increase and abound in love to one another and to all . . . so that He may establish your hearts blameless in holiness before our God and Father at the coming of our Lord Jesus Christ with all His saints (1 Thessalonians 3:12-13, NKJV).

➢ *Takeaway* **May the Lord make you increase and abound in love.**

POWERTHOUGHT How can the heavenly Father answer prayers we do not pray?

Thirty-Five

IS THERE LIFE AFTER DEATH?

☐ 239

Jesus told her, "I am the one who raises the dead and gives them life again. Anyone who believes in me, even though he dies like anyone else, shall live again. He is given eternal life for believing in me and shall never perish" (John 11:25-26).

➢ *Takeaway* **Anyone who believes in me, even though he dies like anyone else, shall live again.**

☐ 240

God has reserved for his children the priceless gift of eternal life; it is kept in heaven for you, pure and undefiled, beyond the reach of change and decay. And God, in his mighty power, will make sure that you get there safely to receive it because you are trusting him. It will be yours in that coming last day for all to see (1 Peter 1:4-5).

➢ *Takeaway* **The priceless gift of eternal life is kept in heaven for you, pure and undefiled, beyond the reach of change and decay.**

☐ 241 ______________________________

These earthly bodies make us groan and sigh. . . . We want to slip into our new bodies so that these dying bodies will, as it were, be swallowed up by everlasting life. This is what God has prepared for us, and as a guarantee he has given us his Holy Spirit. Now we look forward with confidence to our heavenly bodies, realizing that every moment we spend in these earthly bodies is time spent away from our eternal home in heaven with Jesus. We know these things are true by believing, not by seeing. And we are not afraid but are quite content to die, for then we will be at home with the Lord (2 Corinthians 5:4-8).

➢ *Takeaway* **We are quite content to die, for then we will be at home with the Lord.**

☐ 242 ______

This Good News tells us that God makes us ready for heaven—makes us right in God's sight—when we put our faith and trust in Christ to save us. This is accomplished from start to finish by faith. As the Scripture says it, "The man who finds life will find it through trusting God" (Romans 1:17).

➢ *Takeaway* **God makes us ready for heaven when we put our faith and trust in Christ to save us.**

☐ 243 ______

All creation is waiting patiently and hopefully for that future day when God will resurrect his children. For on that day thorns and thistles, sin, death, and decay . . . will all disappear, and the world around us will share in the glorious freedom from sin which God's children enjoy (Romans 8:19-21).

➢ *Takeaway* **On that future day when God will resurrect his children, thorns and thistles, sin, death, and decay will all disappear.**

☐ 244 ______

What is it that God has said? That he has given us eternal life and that this life is in his Son. . . . Everyone dies because all of us are related to Adam, being members of his sinful race, and wherever there is sin, death results. But all who are related to Christ will rise again (1 John 5:11; 1 Corinthians 15:22).

➢ *Takeaway* **All who are related to Christ will rise again.**

☐ 245 ___

We know that when this tent we live in now is taken down—when we die and leave these bodies—we will have wonderful new bodies in heaven, homes that will be ours forevermore, made for us by God himself and not by human hands. . . . If the Spirit of God, who raised up Jesus from the dead, lives in you, he will make your dying bodies live again after you die, by means of this same Holy Spirit living within you (2 Corinthians 5:1; Romans 8:11).

➢ *Takeaway* **We know that when we die and leave these bodies, we will have wonderful new bodies in heaven.**

POWERTHOUGHT Don't be afraid, little flock. For it gives your Father great happiness to give you the Kingdom (Luke 12:32).

Thirty-Six

GETTING ALONG WITH OTHER PEOPLE

☐ 246

Be gentle and ready to forgive; never hold grudges. Remember, the Lord forgave you, so you must forgive others (Colossians 3:13).

➢ *Takeaway* **Be gentle and ready to forgive.**

☐ 247

He who is slow to anger is better than the mighty, and he who rules his spirit, than he who captures a city (Proverbs 16:32, NASB).

➢ *Takeaway* **He who rules his spirit is better than he who captures a city.**

☐ 248 ______

A cheerful heart does good like medicine, but a broken spirit makes one sick (Proverbs 17:22).

➢ *Takeaway* **A cheerful heart does good like medicine.**

☐ 249 ______

A man who hardens his neck after much reproof will suddenly be broken beyond remedy. . . . A fool always loses his temper, but a wise man holds it back. . . . A man's pride will bring him low, but a humble spirit will obtain honor (Proverbs 29:1, 11, 23, NASB).

➢ *Takeaway* **A fool always loses his temper; a wise man holds it back.**

☐ 250 ______

A lazy fellow is a pain to his employers—like smoke in their eyes or vinegar that sets the teeth on edge (Proverbs 10:26).

➢ *Takeaway* **A lazy fellow is like vinegar that sets the teeth on edge.**

☐ 251 ______

Don't grumble about each other, brothers. Are you yourselves above criticism? For see! The great Judge is coming. He is almost here. [Let him do whatever criticizing must be done.] . . . Gentle words cause life and health; griping brings discouragement (James 5:9; Proverbs 15:4).

➢ *Takeaway* **Let the great Judge do whatever criticizing must be done.**

☐ 252 ______________________________

Learn to put aside your own desires so that you will become patient and godly, gladly letting God have his way with you. This will make possible the next step, which is for you to enjoy other people and to like them, and finally you will grow to love them deeply (2 Peter 1:6-7).

➢ *Takeaway* **Learn to put aside your own desires so that you will become patient and godly.**

POWERTHOUGHT To wrong those we hate is to add fuel to our hatred. Conversely, to treat an enemy with magnanimity is to blunt our hatred for him.

—Eric Hoffer

Thirty-Seven

HOW TO GET ALONG WITH OTHER PEOPLE

☐ 253 ______________________________

Don't be selfish; don't live to make a good impression on others. Be humble, thinking of others as better than yourself. Don't just think about your own affairs, but be interested in others, too, and in what they are doing (Philippians 2:3-4).

➢ *Takeaway* **Don't live to make a good impression on others.**

☐ 254 ______________________________

Do not be haughty in mind, but associate with the lowly. Do not be wise in your own estimation. Never pay back evil for evil to anyone. . . . If possible, so far as it depends on you, be at peace with all men (Romans 12:16-18, NASB).

➢ *Takeaway* **Do not be wise in your own estimation.**

☐ 255

In everything you do, stay away from complaining and arguing. . . . You are to live clean, innocent lives as children of God in a dark world full of people who are crooked and stubborn. Shine out among them like beacon lights (Philippians 2:14-15).

➢ *Takeaway* **In everything you do, stay away from complaining and arguing.**

☐ 256

Forgive men their transgressions. . . . Do not judge lest you be judged. For in the way you judge, you will be judged; and by your standard of measure, it will be measured to you. And why do you look at the speck that is in your brother's eye, but do not notice the log that is in your own eye? (Matthew 6:14; 7:1-3, NASB).

➢ *Takeaway* **Why do you look at the speck that is in your brother's eye, but do not notice the log that is in your own eye?**

☐ 257 ______

Love forgets mistakes; nagging about them parts the best of friends (Proverbs 17:9).

➢ *Takeaway* **Love forgets mistakes.**

☐ 258 ______

A relaxed attitude lengthens a man's life; jealousy rots it away. . . . It is best to listen much, speak little, and not become angry (Proverbs 14:30; James 1:19).

➢ *Takeaway* **A relaxed attitude lengthens a man's life.**

☐ 259 ______

The wisdom that comes from heaven is first of all pure and full of quiet gentleness. Then it is peace-loving and courteous. It allows discussion and is willing to yield to others; it is full of mercy and good deeds. It is wholehearted and straightforward and sincere (James 3:17).

➢ *Takeaway* **The wisdom that comes from heaven allows discussion.**

POWERTHOUGHT Lord, help me to realize how brief my time on earth will be. Help me to know that I am here for but a moment more. . . . Save me from being overpowered by my sins (Psalm 39:4, 8).

Thirty-Eight

WHAT IS REAL LOVE?

☐ 260 ________________________________

Love is patient, love is kind. It does not envy, it does not boast, it is not proud. It is not rude, it is not self-seeking, it is not easily angered, it keeps no record of wrongs (1 Corinthians 13:4-5, NIV).

➢ *Takeaway* **Love is patient, love is kind. It keeps no record of wrongs.**

☐ 261 ________________________________

[Love] is never glad about injustice, but rejoices whenever truth wins out. If you love someone, you will be loyal to him no matter what the cost. You will always believe in him, always expect the best of him, and always stand your ground in defending him. . . . There are three things that remain—faith, hope, and love—and the greatest of these is love (1 Corinthians 13:6-7, 13).

➢ *Takeaway* **Love is never glad about injustice.**

☐ 262 ______________________________

Do nothing out of selfish ambition or vain conceit, but in humility consider others better than yourselves. Each of you should look not only to your own interests, but also to the interests of others. Your attitude should be the same as that of Christ Jesus: who . . . made himself nothing, taking the very nature of a servant (Philippians 2:3-7, NIV).

➢ *Takeaway* **Consider others better than yourselves.**

☐ 263 ______________________________

God is love, and anyone who lives in love is living with God and God is living in him. . . . If anyone says "I love God," but keeps on hating his brother, he is a liar. . . . God himself has said that one must love not only God, but his brother too (1 John 4:16, 20-21).

➢ *Takeaway* **God has said that one must love not only God, but his brother too.**

☐ 264 ________________________________

If you suffer for doing good and you endure it, this is commendable before God. To this you were called, because Christ suffered for you, leaving you an example, that you should follow in his steps (1 Peter 2:20-21, NIV).

➢ *Takeaway* **If you suffer for doing good, this is commendable before God.**

☐ 265 ________________________________

If you obey my commands, you will remain in my love. . . . My command is this: Love each other as I have loved you. Greater love has no one than this, that he lay down his life for his friends. . . . I chose you . . . to go and bear fruit—fruit that will last. . . . Love each other (John 15:10, 12-13, 16-17, NIV).

➢ *Takeaway* **Greater love has no one than this, that he lay down his life for his friends.**

☐ 266 ________________________________

God showed how much he loved us by sending his only Son into this wicked world to bring to us eternal life through his death. In this act we see what real love is. . . . Our love for him comes as a result of his loving us first (1 John 4:9-10, 19).

➢ *Takeaway* **God sent his only Son. In this act we see what real love is.**

POWERTHOUGHT Some day after mastering the wind, the waves, the tides and gravity, we shall harness for God the energies of love. And then, for the second time in the history of the world, man will have discovered fire.

—Teilhard de Chardin

Thirty-Nine

YOU CAN TRUST GOD; HE LOVES YOU

☐ 267

He is like a father to us, tender and sympathetic to those who reverence him. For he knows we are but dust and that our days are few and brief, like grass, like flowers, blown by the wind and gone forever. But the loving-kindness of the Lord is from everlasting to everlasting to those who reverence him (Psalm 103:13-18).

➢ *Takeaway* **He is like a father to us, tender and sympathetic, for he knows we are**

but dust and that our days are few and brief, like grass, like flowers.

☐ 268 ______________________________

I pray that you, being rooted and established in love, may have power, together with all the saints, to grasp how wide and long and high and deep is the love of Christ, and to know this love that surpasses knowledge—that you may be filled to the measure of all the fullness of God (Ephesians 3:17-19, NIV).

➢ *Takeaway* **Grasp how wide and long and high and deep is the love of Christ.**

☐ 269 ______________________________

What, then, shall we say in response to this? If God is for us, who can be against us? He who did not spare his own Son, but gave him up for us all—how will he not also, along with him, graciously give us all things? (Romans 8:31-32, NIV).

➢ *Takeaway* **If God is for us, who can be against us?**

☐ 270 ______________________________

Comfort, comfort my people, says your God. . . . He tends his flock like a shepherd: He gathers the lambs in his arms and carries them close to his heart; he gently leads those that have young (Isaiah 40:1, 11, NIV).

➢ *Takeaway* **He gathers the lambs in his arms and carries them close to his heart.**

☐ 271 ______________________________

I am convinced that neither death nor life, neither angels nor demons, neither the present nor the future, nor any powers, neither height nor depth, nor anything else in all creation, will be able to separate us from the love of God that is in Christ Jesus our Lord (Romans 8:38-39, NIV).

➢ *Takeaway* **I am convinced that neither death nor life, neither angels nor demons, neither the present nor the future, nor any powers, will be able to separate us from the love of God.**

☐ 272 ______________________________

I will say of the LORD, "He is my refuge and my fortress, my God, in whom I trust.". . . He will cover you with his feathers, and under his wings you will find refuge; his faithfulness will be your shield and rampart (Psalm 91:2, 4, NIV).

➢ *Takeaway* **Under his wings you will find refuge.**

☐ 273 ______________________________

Cast your burden on the LORD, and He shall sustain you; He shall never permit the righteous to be moved (Psalm 55:22, NKJV).

➢ *Takeaway* **Cast your burden on the LORD.**

POWERTHOUGHT If you are sure it is a right thing for which you are asking, plead now, plead at noon, plead at night, plead on with cries and tears. Spread out your case. Order your arguments. Back up your pleas with reasons. Urge the precious blood of Jesus.

—Charles Haddon Spurgeon

Forty

COMFORT IN TIMES OF FAILURE

☐ 274

My protection and success come from God alone. He is my refuge, a Rock where no enemy can reach me. . . . Trust him all the time. Pour out your longings before him, for he can help! . . . The Lord says, "Don't be afraid. . . . For the battle is not yours, but God's!" . . . He has showered down upon us the richness of his grace—for how well he understands us and knows what is best for us at all times (Psalm 62:7-8; 2 Chronicles 20:15; Ephesians 1:8).

➢ *Takeaway* **My protection and success come from God alone.**

☐ 275 ________________________________

There is none like the God of Jerusalem—he descends from the heavens in majestic splendor to help you. The eternal God is your Refuge, and underneath are the everlasting arms (Deuteronomy 33:26-27).

➢ *Takeaway* **Underneath are the everlasting arms.**

☐ 276 ________________________________

The steps of good men are directed by the Lord. He delights in each step they take. If they fall it isn't fatal, for the Lord holds them with his hand. . . . We know that all that happens to us is working for our good if we love God and are fitting into his plans (Psalm 37:23-24; Romans 8:28).

➢ *Takeaway* **All that happens to us is working for our good if we love God.**

☐ 277 ________________________________

Be truly glad! There is wonderful joy ahead, even though the going is rough for a while down here. These trials are only to test your faith, to see whether or not it is strong and pure. It is being tested as fire tests gold and purifies it—and your faith is far more precious to God than mere gold; so if your faith remains strong after being tried in the test tube of fiery trials, it will bring you much praise and glory and honor on the day of his return (1 Peter 1:6-7).

➢ *Takeaway* **There is wonderful joy ahead, even though the going is rough for a while down here.**

☐ 278 ______________________________

You love me! You are holding my right hand! You will keep on guiding me all my life with your wisdom and counsel, and afterwards receive me into the glories of heaven! Whom have I in heaven but you? And I desire no one on earth as much as you! My health fails; my spirits droop, yet God remains! He is the strength of my heart; he is mine forever! (Psalm 73:23-26).

➢ *Takeaway* **You love me! You are holding my right hand!**

☐ 279 ______________________________

Everything in the heavens and earth is yours, O Lord, and this is your kingdom. We adore you as being in control of everything. Riches and honor come from you alone, and you are the Ruler of all mankind; your hand controls power and might, and it is at your discretion that men are made great and given strength. O our God, we thank you and praise your glorious name (1 Chronicles 29:11-13).

➢ *Takeaway* **Your hand controls power and might, and it is at your discretion that men are made great and given strength.**

☐ 280

Don't you know by now that the everlasting God, the Creator of the farthest parts of the earth, never grows faint or weary? No one can fathom the depths of his understanding. He gives power to the tired and worn out, and strength to the weak. . . . They that wait upon the Lord shall renew their strength. They shall mount up with wings like eagles; they shall run and not be weary; they shall walk and not faint (Isaiah 40:28-29, 31).

➢ *Takeaway* **He gives power to the tired and worn out, and strength to the weak.**

POWERTHOUGHT God tempers the wind to the shorn lamb.

—Henri Estienne

Forty-One

MAKING DECISIONS

☐ 281 ______

I advise you to obey only the Holy Spirit's instructions. He will tell you where to go and what to do. . . . Follow the Holy Spirit's leading. . . . Then we won't need to look for honors and popularity, which lead to jealousy and hard feelings (Galatians 5:16, 25-26).

➢ *Takeaway* **Follow the Holy Spirit's leading.**

☐ 282 ______

We can make our plans, but the final outcome is in God's hands. . . . Commit your work to the Lord, then it will succeed. . . . The Lord demands fairness in every business deal. He established this principle (Proverbs 16:1, 3, 11).

➢ *Takeaway* **The Lord demands fairness. He established this principle.**

☐ 283

If any of you lacks wisdom, let him ask of God, who gives to all men generously and without reproach, and it will be given to him. But let him ask in faith without any doubting, for the one who doubts is like the surf of the sea driven and tossed by the wind (James 1:5-6, NASB).

➢ *Takeaway* **If any of you lacks wisdom, let him ask of God.**

☐ 284

Let everyone who is godly pray to Thee in a time when Thou mayest be found. . . . I will instruct you and teach you in the way which you should go; I will counsel you with My eye upon you (Psalm 32:6, 8, NASB).

➢ *Takeaway* **I will instruct you and teach you in the way which you should go.**

☐ 285

Timely advice is as lovely as gold apples in a silver basket. . . . If you profit from constructive criticism, you will be elected to the wise men's hall of fame. But to reject criticism is to harm yourself and your own best interests (Proverbs 25:11; 15:31-32).

➢ *Takeaway* **Profit from constructive criticism.**

☐ 286 ______________________________

Thy commandments make me wiser than my enemies. . . . I understand more than the aged, because I have observed Thy precepts. . . . Thy word is a lamp to my feet, and a light to my path (Psalm 119:98, 100, 105, NASB).

➢ *Takeaway* **Thy word is a light to my path.**

☐ 287 ______________________________

Never tire of loyalty and kindness. Hold these virtues tightly. . . . In everything you do, put God first, and he will direct you and crown your efforts with success (Proverbs 3:3, 6).

➢ *Takeaway* **Never tire of loyalty and kindness. Hold these virtues tightly.**

POWERTHOUGHT If you want better insight and discernment, and are searching for them as you would for lost money or hidden treasure, then wisdom will be given you. . . . For the Lord grants wisdom! . . . He grants good sense to the godly—his saints. He is their shield, protecting them and guarding their pathway. He shows how to distinguish right from wrong, how to find the right decision every time. . . . Wisdom and truth will enter the very center of your being, filling your life with joy (Proverbs 2:3, 6-10).

Forty-Two

FINDING GOD'S PEACE

☐ 288 ______________________________

Christ's death on the cross has made peace with God for all by his blood. This includes you who were once so far away from God. . . . Now he has brought you back as his friends. . . . Christ has brought you into the very presence of God, and you are standing there before him with nothing left against you—nothing left that he could even chide you for (Colossians 1:20-22).

➢ *Takeaway* **Christ's death on the cross has made peace with God for all by his blood.**

☐ 289 ______________________________

Wait on the LORD, and keep His way, and He shall exalt you. . . . Mark the blameless man, and observe the upright; for the future of that man is peace. . . . The salvation of the righteous is from the LORD; He is their strength in the time of trouble (Psalm 37:34, 37, 39, NKJV).

➢ *Takeaway* **Mark the blameless man, and observe the upright; for the future of that man is peace.**

☐ 290 ______________________________

When a man is trying to please God, God makes even his worst enemies to be at peace with him. . . . Try always to be led along together by the Holy Spirit and so be at peace with one another (Proverbs 16:7; Ephesians 4:3).

➢ *Takeaway* **Be at peace with one another.**

☐ 291 ______________________________

He will keep in perfect peace all those who trust in him, whose thoughts turn often to the Lord! . . . What can we ever say to such wonderful things as these? If God is on our side, who can ever be against us? (Isaiah 26:3; Romans 8:31).

➢ *Takeaway* **He will keep in perfect peace all those who trust him.**

☐ 292 ________________________________

In the last days Mount Zion will be the most renowned of all the mountains of the world. . . . In those days the whole world will be ruled by the Lord from Jerusalem! . . . He will arbitrate among the nations and dictate to strong nations far away. They will beat their swords into plowshares and their spears into pruning-hooks; nations shall no longer fight each other, for all war will end. There will be universal peace, and all the military academies and training camps will be closed down. Everyone will live quietly in his own home in peace and prosperity, for there will be nothing to fear (Micah 4:1-4).

➢ *Takeaway* **In the last days the whole world will be ruled by the Lord from Jerusalem. Nations shall no longer fight each other.**

☐ 293 ________________________________

The Lord pleads with you still: Ask where the good road is, the godly paths you used to walk in, in the days of long ago. Travel there, and you will find rest for your souls (Jeremiah 6:16).

➢ *Takeaway* **The godly paths . . . travel there, and you will find rest for your souls.**

☐ 294 ______________________________

Never envy the wicked! Soon they fade away like grass and disappear. Trust in the Lord instead. Be kind and good to others. . . . All who humble themselves before the Lord shall be given every blessing and shall have wonderful peace (Psalm 37:1-3, 11).

➢ *Takeaway* **Be kind and good to others. All who humble themselves before the Lord shall have wonderful peace.**

POWERTHOUGHT If we had no winter, the spring would not be so pleasant.

—Anne Bradstreet, 1664

Forty-Three

WAITING AND TRUSTING

☐ 295 ______________________________

Look at the birds of the air, for they neither sow nor reap nor gather into barns; yet your heavenly Father feeds them. Are you not of more value than they? Which of you by worrying can add one cubit to his stature? . . . If God so clothes the grass of the field, which today is, and tomorrow is thrown into the oven, will He not much more clothe you, O you of little faith? . . . Seek first the kingdom of God and His righteousness, and all these things shall be added to you (Matthew 6:26-27, 30, 33, NKJV).

➢ *Takeaway* **Which of you by worrying can add one cubit to his stature?**

☐ 296 ______________________________

I will cry to the God of heaven who does such wonders for me. He will send down help from heaven to save me because of his love and his faithfulness. He will rescue me. . . . O God, my heart is quiet and confident. No wonder I can sing your praises! . . . Your kindness and love are as vast as the heavens. Your faithfulness is higher than the skies (Psalm 57:2-3, 7, 10).

➢ *Takeaway* **Your kindness and love are as vast as the heavens. Your faithfulness is higher than the skies.**

☐ 297 ______________________________

Your faith and hope can rest in him alone. . . . When you draw close to God, God will draw close to you. . . . The Lord my God is my fortress—the mighty Rock where I can hide (1 Peter 1:21; James 4:8; Psalm 94:22).

➢ *Takeaway* **The Lord my God is my fortress—the mighty Rock where I can hide.**

☐ 298 ______________________________

God is our refuge and strength, an ever-present help in trouble. Therefore we will not fear, though the earth give way and the mountains fall into the heart of the sea, though its waters roar and foam and the mountains quake with their surging. . . . Nations are in uproar, kingdoms fall; he lifts his voice, the earth melts. . . . Be still, and know that I am God; I will be exalted among the nations. . . . The LORD Almighty is with us; the God of Jacob is our fortress (Psalm 46:1-3, 6, 10-11, NIV).

➢ *Takeaway* **Be still, and know that I am God.**

☐ 299 ______________________________

If it had not been the LORD who was on our side, when men rose up against us, then they would have swallowed us alive. . . . The waters would have overwhelmed us, the stream would have gone over our soul. . . . Blessed be the LORD. . . . Our soul has escaped as a bird from the snare of the fowlers. . . . Our help is in the name of the LORD, who made heaven and earth (Psalm 124:2-8, NKJV).

➢ *Takeaway* **Our help is in the name of the Lord.**

☐ 300 ______________________________

Praise the Lord! For all who fear God and trust in him are blessed beyond expression. Yes, happy is the man who delights in doing his commands. . . . When darkness overtakes him, light will come bursting in. . . . He does not fear bad news, nor live in dread of what may happen. For he is settled in his mind that Jehovah will take care of him (Psalm 112:1, 4, 7).

➢ *Takeaway* **All who fear God and trust in him do not fear bad news, nor live in dread of what may happen.**

☐ 301 ______

The angel of the LORD encamps all around those who fear Him, and delivers them. Oh, taste and see that the LORD is good. . . . Those who seek the LORD shall not lack any good thing (Psalm 34:7-8, 10, NKJV).

➢ *Takeaway* **The angel of the Lord encamps all around those who fear him.**

POWER THOUGHT There is no unbelief; whoever plants a seed beneath the sod and waits to see it push away the clod trusts in God.

—Edward Bulwer-Lytton

Forty-Four

WHAT IS GOD LIKE?

☐ 302

In [Christ] are hidden all the treasures of wisdom and knowledge. . . . Now to the King eternal, immortal, invisible, to God who alone is wise, be honor and glory forever and ever. Amen (Colossians 2:3; 1 Timothy 1:17, NKJV).

➢ *Takeaway* **In him are hidden all the treasures of wisdom and knowledge.**

☐ 303

Who else has held the oceans in his hands and measured off the heavens with his ruler? Who else knows the weight of all the earth and weighs the mountains and the hills? . . . All the peoples of the world are nothing in comparison with him—they are but a drop in the bucket, dust on the scales. He picks up the islands as though they had no weight at all. All of Lebanon's forests do not contain sufficient fuel to consume a sacrifice large enough to honor him, nor are all its animals enough to offer to our God (Isaiah 40:12, 15-16).

➢ *Takeaway* **All of Lebanon's forests do not contain sufficient fuel to consume a sacrifice large enough to honor him.**

☐ 304

He made the world and everything in it, and since he is Lord of heaven and earth, he doesn't live in man-made temples; and human hands can't minister to his needs—for he has no needs! He himself gives life and breath to everything, and satisfies every need there is. He created all the people of the world from one man, Adam, and scattered the nations across the face of the earth. He decided beforehand which should rise and fall, and when. He determined their boundaries (Acts 17:24-26).

➢ *Takeaway* **He scattered the nations across the face of the earth. He decided beforehand which should rise and fall, and when.**

☐ 305 ______________________________

You are God without beginning or end. . . . A thousand years are but as yesterday to you! They are like a single hour! (Psalm 90:2, 4).

➢ *Takeaway* **A thousand years are but as yesterday to you!**

☐ 306 ______________________________

Seek him who created the Seven Stars and the constellation Orion, who turns darkness into morning and day into night, who calls forth the water from the ocean and pours it out as rain upon land. The Lord, Jehovah, is his name (Amos 5:8).

➢ *Takeaway* **Seek him who created the Seven Stars and the constellation Orion.**

☐ 307 ______________________________

It is God who sits above the circle of the earth. . . . He dooms the great men of the world and brings them all to naught. They hardly get started, barely take root, when he blows on them and their work withers, and the wind carries them off like straw. "With whom will you compare me? Who is my equal?" asks the Holy One. Look up into the heavens! Who created all these stars? As a shepherd leads his sheep, calling each by its pet name, and counts them to see that none are lost or strayed, so God does with stars and planets! (Isaiah 40:22-26).

➢ *Takeaway* **As a shepherd leads his sheep, calling each by its pet name, so God does with stars and planets!**

☐ 308 ______________________________

Who else but God goes back and forth to heaven? Who else holds the wind in his fists and wraps up the oceans in his cloak? Who but God has created the world? If there is any other, what is his name—and his Son's name—if you know it? (Proverbs 30:4).

➢ *Takeaway* **Who else holds the wind in his fists and wraps up the oceans in his cloak?**

POWERTHOUGHT If the stars should appear one night in a thousand years, how men would believe and adore!

—Ralph Waldo Emerson

Forty-Five

IS YOUR GOD TOO SMALL?

☐ 309 ______________________

He formed the mountains by his mighty strength. He quiets the raging oceans and all the world's clamor. In the farthest corners of the earth the glorious acts of God shall startle everyone. . . . He waters the earth to make it fertile. . . . Then he crowns it all with green, lush pastures in the wilderness; hillsides blossom with joy. The pastures are filled with flocks of sheep, and the valleys are carpeted with grain. All the world shouts with joy and sings (Psalm 65:6-9, 11-13).

➢ *Takeaway* **The glorious acts of God shall startle everyone.**

☐ 310 ________________________________

How great are God's riches! How deep are his wisdom and knowledge! Who can explain his decisions? Who can understand his ways? As the scripture says, "Who knows the mind of the Lord? Who is able to give him advice? Who has ever given him anything, so that he had to pay it back?" For all things were created by him, and all things exist through him and for him. To God be the glory forever! Amen (Romans 11:33-36, TEV).

➢ *Takeaway* **How deep are his wisdom and knowledge!**

☐ 311 ________________________________

I . . . saw—oh, the glory of it!—a throne and someone sitting on it! Great bursts of light flashed forth from him as from a glittering diamond or from a shining ruby, and a rainbow glowing like an emerald encircled his throne. . . . Lightning and thunder issued from the throne, and there were voices in the thunder. . . . Spread out before it was a shiny crystal sea. . . . Day after day . . . they kept on saying, "Holy, holy, holy, Lord God Almighty—the one who was, and is, and is to come." . . . The Lord is in his holy Temple; let all the earth be silent before him (Revelation 4:2-3, 5-6, 8; Habakkuk 2:20).

➢ *Takeaway* **Day after day they kept on saying, "Holy, holy, holy, Lord God**

Almighty—the one who was, and is, and is to come."

☐ 312

Jesus said to his disciples, "Let us go across to the other side of the lake." . . . Suddenly a strong wind blew up, and the waves began to spill over into the boat, so that it was about to fill with water. Jesus was in the back of the boat, sleeping with his head on a pillow. The disciples woke him up and said, "Teacher, don't you care that we are about to die?" Jesus stood up and commanded the wind, "Be quiet!" and he said to the waves, "Be still!" The wind died down, and there was a great calm. . . . [The disciples] began to say to one another, "Who is this man? Even the wind and the waves obey him!" (Mark 4:35, 37-39, 41, TEV).

➢ *Takeaway* **Even the wind and the waves obey him!**

☐ 313

The LORD is king. He is clothed with majesty and strength. The earth is set firmly in place and cannot be moved. Your throne, O LORD, has been firm from the beginning, and you existed before time began. . . . The LORD rules supreme in heaven, greater than the roar of the ocean, more powerful than the waves of the sea (Psalm 93:1-2, 4, TEV).

➢ *Takeaway* **The Lord rules supreme in heaven, more powerful than the waves of the sea.**

☐ 314 ____________________

O Jehovah, Commander of the heavenly armies, where is there any other Mighty One like you? Faithfulness is your very character. You rule the oceans when their waves arise in fearful storms; you speak, and they lie still. . . . The heavens are yours, the world, everything—for you created them all. . . . Strong is your arm! Strong is your hand! . . . Your throne is founded on two strong pillars—the one is Justice and the other Righteousness. Mercy and Truth walk before you as your attendants (Psalm 89:8-11, 13-14).

➢ *Takeaway* **Jehovah, Commander of the heavenly armies, faithfulness is your very character.**

☐ 315 ____________________

It is God who directs the lives of his creatures; every man's life is in his power. . . . Drought comes when God withholds rain; floods come when he turns water loose. God is strong and always victorious; both deceived and deceiver are in his power. He takes away the wisdom of rulers. . . . He dethrones kings and makes them prisoners. . . . He sends light to places dark as death. He makes nations strong and great, but then he defeats and destroys them (Job 12:10, 15-18, 22-23, TEV).

➢ *Takeaway* **Both deceived and deceiver are in his power.**

POWERTHOUGHT Isn't God wonderful?

Forty-Six

IS JESUS GOD?

☐ 316 ______________________________

The Jewish leaders surrounded him [Jesus] and asked, ". . . If you are the Messiah, tell us plainly." "I have already told you, and you don't believe me," Jesus replied. "The proof is in the miracles I do in the name of my Father. . . . I and the Father are one" (John 10:24-25, 30).

➢ *Takeaway* **I and the Father are one. The proof is in the miracles I do.**

☐ 317 ______________________________

Before anything else existed, there was Christ, with God. He has always been alive and is himself

God. He created everything there is—nothing exists that he didn't make. Eternal life is in him, and this life gives light to all mankind. . . . I . . . testify that he is the Son of God (John 1:1-4, 34).

➢ *Takeaway* **I testify that he is the Son of God.**

☐ 318 ____________________

[Jesus Christ] laid aside his mighty power and glory, taking the disguise of a slave and becoming like men. And he humbled himself even further, going so far as actually to die a criminal's death on a cross. Yet it was because of this that God raised him up to the heights of heaven and gave him a name which is above every other name, that at the name of Jesus every knee shall bow in heaven and on earth and under the earth, and every tongue shall confess that Jesus Christ is Lord, to the glory of God the Father (Philippians 2:7-11).

➢ *Takeaway* **At the name of Jesus every knee shall bow in heaven and on earth and under the earth, and every tongue shall confess that Jesus Christ is Lord.**

☐ 319 ____________________

O Bethlehem Ephrathah, you are but a small Judean village, yet you will be the birthplace of my King who is alive from everlasting ages past! . . . Jesus was born in the town of Bethlehem, in Judea, during the reign of King Herod. . . . This is what the prophet Micah wrote: "O little town of Bethlehem, you are not just an unimportant Judean village, for a Governor shall rise from you to rule my people Israel" (Micah 5:2; Matthew 2:1, 5-6).

➢ *Takeaway* **O little town of Bethlehem, you are not just an unimportant Judean village, for a Governor shall rise from you.**

☐ 320 ______________________________

Taking [the disciples] aside, Jesus once more began describing all that was going to happen to him when they arrived at Jerusalem. "When we get there," he told them, "I, the Messiah, will be arrested and taken before the chief priests and the Jewish leaders, who will sentence me to die and hand me over to the Romans to be killed. They will mock me and spit on me and flog me with their whips and kill me; but after three days I will come back to life again." . . . Don't ever forget the wonderful fact that Jesus Christ was a man, born into King David's family; and that he was God, as shown by the fact that he rose again from the dead (Mark 10:32-34; 2 Timothy 2:8).

➢ *Takeaway* **He was God as shown by the fact that he rose from the dead.**

☐ 321 ______________________________

Christ died for our sins just as the Scriptures said he would, . . . he was buried, and . . . three days afterwards he arose from the grave just as the prophets foretold. He was seen by Peter and later by the rest of "the Twelve." After that he was seen by more than five hundred Christian brothers at one time (1 Corinthians 15:3-6).

➢ *Takeaway* **He arose from the grave just as the prophets foretold, and after that he was seen by more than five hundred.**

☐ 322

My own eyes have seen his splendor and his glory: I was there on the holy mountain when he shone out with honor given him by God his Father; I heard that glorious, majestic voice calling down from heaven, saying, "This is my much-loved Son; I am well pleased with him." So we have seen and proved that what the prophets said came true (2 Peter 1:16-19).

➢ *Takeaway* **This is my much-loved Son; I am well pleased with him.**

POWERTHOUGHT I believe I am walking testimony that Jesus Christ was raised from the dead and lives today. I set out to intellectually refute the Resurrection and Christianity. After gathering the evidence, I was compelled to conclude that my arguments wouldn't stand up, that Jesus Christ was exactly who he claimed to be—the Son of God.

—Josh McDowell, ***The Resurrection Factor***

Forty-Seven

IS JESUS GOD? THE EVIDENCE:

☐ 323 ________________________________

(What John said)
God showed how much he loved us by sending his only Son into this wicked world to bring to us eternal life through his death. . . . And furthermore, we have seen with our own eyes and now tell all the world that God sent his Son to be their Savior (1 John 4:9, 14).

➢ *Takeaway* **We have seen with our own eyes and now tell all the world that God sent his Son.**

☐ 324 ________________________________

(What Jesus said)
I am the way, the truth, and the life. No one comes to the Father except through Me. . . . He who has seen Me has seen the Father. . . . Believe Me that I am in the Father and the Father in Me; or else believe Me for the sake of the works themselves (John 14:6, 9, 11, NKJV).

➢ *Takeaway* **He who has seen me has seen the Father.**

☐ 325 ________________________________

[Christ] is the image of the invisible God, the first-born over all creation. For by Him all things were created that are in heaven and that are on earth, visible and invisible, whether thrones or dominions or principalities or powers. All things were created through Him and for Him. And He is before all things, and in Him all things consist (Colossians 1:15-17,NKJV).

➢ *Takeaway* **Christ is the image of the invisible God. All things were created through Him.**

☐ 326 ________________________________

[Jesus] taught His disciples and said to them, "The Son of Man is being betrayed into the hands of men, and they will kill Him. And after He is killed, He will rise the third day." But they did not understand this saying (Mark 9:31-31, NKJV).

➢ *Takeaway* **He taught his disciples that he will rise the third day.**

☐ 327 ______________________________

(Words from Jesus)
If you trust me, you are really trusting God. For when you see me, you are seeing the one who sent me. . . . All who reject me and my message will be judged at the Day of Judgment by the truths I have spoken (John 12:44-45, 48).

➢ *Takeaway* **If you trust me, you are really trusting God.**

☐ 328 ______________________________

(Isaiah predicted Jesus' coming centuries before)
For to us a child is born, to us a son is given, and the government will be on his shoulders. And he will be called Wonderful Counselor, Mighty God, Everlasting Father, Prince of Peace. Of the increase of his government and peace there will be no end (Isaiah 9:6-7, NIV).

➢ *Takeaway* **Unto us a child is born, and he will be called Mighty God, Everlasting Father, Prince of Peace.**

☐ 329 ______________________________

(Isaiah: about 700 years B.C.)
The Lord himself will choose the sign—a child shall be born to a virgin! And she shall call him Immanuel (meaning, "God is with us"). . . . See my

servant . . . my Chosen One in whom I delight. I have put my Spirit upon him; he will reveal justice to the nations of the world. . . . He won't be satisfied until truth and righteousness prevail throughout the earth, nor until even distant lands beyond the seas have put their trust in him (Isaiah 7:14; 42:1, 4).

➢ *Takeaway* **A child shall be born to a virgin, and she shall call him Immanuel, (meaning, "God is with us").**

POWERTHOUGHT

What seems to be a stumbling block may be a stepping-stone;
What seems to be a solid wall may be a door unknown;
What seems to be a speck of dust may be, in truth, pure gold;
So walk by faith and not by sight, no good will God withhold.

—Phillis C. Michael, *Decision* magazine, June 1982

Forty-Eight

PROMISES TO CLAIM

☐ 330 ______

The godly shall flourish like palm trees and grow tall as the cedars of Lebanon. For they are transplanted into the Lord's own garden and are under his personal care. Even in old age they will still produce fruit and be vital and green (Psalm 92:12-14).

➢ *Takeaway* **The godly shall flourish like palm trees. They are under his personal care.**

☐ 331 ______________________________

God has made the sins of evil men to boomerang upon them! He will destroy them by their own plans. Jehovah our God will cut them off. . . . The Lord continues forever, exalted in the heavens, while his enemies—all evil-doers—shall be scattered (Psalms 94:23; 92:8-9).

➢ *Takeaway* **God has made the sins of evil men to boomerang upon them.**

☐ 332 ______________________________

It is he who will supply all your needs from his riches in glory because of what Christ Jesus has done for us. Now unto God our Father be glory forever and ever. Amen (Philippians 4:19-20).

➢ *Takeaway* **He will supply all your needs.**

☐ 333 ______________________________

When sins have once been forever forgiven and forgotten, there is no need to offer more sacrifices to get rid of them. And so, dear brothers, now we may walk right into the very Holy of Holies, where God is, because of the blood of Jesus (Hebrews 10:18-19).

➢ *Takeaway* **We may walk right into the very Holy of Holies, where God is, because of the blood of Jesus.**

☐ 334 ___

Listen to me, dear brothers: God has chosen poor people to be rich in faith, and the Kingdom of Heaven is theirs, for that is the gift God has promised to all those who love him (James 2:5).

➢ *Takeaway* **The Kingdom of Heaven—that is the gift God has promised to all those who love him.**

☐ 335 ___

Happy is the man who doesn't give in and do wrong when he is tempted, for afterwards he will get as his reward the crown of life that God has promised those who love him. . . . Give yourselves humbly to God. Resist the devil and he will flee from you (James 1:12; 4:7).

➢ *Takeaway* **Resist the devil and he will flee from you.**

☐ 336 ___

The man who knows right from wrong and has good judgment and common sense is happier than the man who is immensely rich! For such wisdom is far more valuable than precious jewels. Nothing else compares with it. Wisdom gives: a long, good life, riches, honor, pleasure, peace (Proverbs 3:13-17).

➢ *Takeaway* **The man who knows right from wrong is happier than the man who is immensely rich!**

POWERTHOUGHT We always pay dearly for chasing after what is cheap.

—Aleksandr Solzhenitsyn

Forty-Nine

LET'S PRAISE GOD TODAY!

☐ 337

I will praise you, O LORD, with all my heart; I will tell of all your wonders. I will be glad and rejoice in you; I will sing praises to your name, O Most High. . . . I will exalt you, O LORD (Psalms 9:1-2; 30:1, NIV).

➢ *Takeaway* **I will exalt you, O LORD.**

☐ 338

The heavens declare the glory of God; the skies proclaim the work of his hands. Day after day they pour forth speech; night after night they display knowledge. There is no speech or language where their voice is not heard (Psalm 19:1-3, NIV).

➢ *Takeaway* **The heavens declare the glory of God.**

☐ 339 ______________________________

Ascribe to the LORD the glory due his name. . . . The voice of the LORD is powerful; the voice of the LORD is majestic. . . . The voice of the LORD breaks in pieces the cedars of Lebanon. . . . The voice of the LORD strikes with flashes of lightning. The voice of the LORD shakes the desert. . . . The voice of the LORD twists the oaks and strips the forests bare. And in his temple all cry, "Glory!" (Psalm 29:2, 4-5, 7-9, NIV).

➢ *Takeaway* **In his temple all cry, "Glory!"**

☐ 340 ______________________________

I will sing of the LORD's great love forever. . . . You rule over the surging sea; when its waves mount up, you still them. . . . You founded the world and all that is in it. You created the north and the south. . . . Your arm is endued with power; your hand is strong, your right hand exalted. Righteousness and justice are the foundation of your throne. . . . Praise be to the LORD forever! Amen and Amen! (Psalm 89:1, 9, 11-14, 52, NIV).

➢ *Takeaway* **You founded the world and all that is in it! Praise be to the LORD forever! Amen and Amen.**

☐ 341 ______________________________

Shout for joy to the LORD, all the earth, burst into jubilant song with music; make music to the LORD with the harp, with the harp and the sound of singing, with trumpets and the blast of the ram's horn—shout for joy before the LORD, the King. Let the sea resound, and everything in it, the world, and all who live in it. Let the rivers clap their hands, let the mountains sing together for joy; let them sing before the LORD (Psalm 98:4-9, NIV).

➢ *Takeaway* **Shout for joy before the LORD, the King.**

☐ 342 ______________________________

Praise the LORD, all you nations; extol him, all you peoples. For great is his love toward us, and the faithfulness of the LORD endures forever. Praise the LORD (Psalm 117, NIV).

➢ *Takeaway* **The faithfulness of the LORD endures forever. Praise the LORD.**

☐ 343 ______________________________

Sing praise to his name. . . . He makes clouds rise from the ends of the earth; he sends lightning with the rain and brings out the wind from his storehouses. . . . He makes grass grow for the cattle, and plants for man to cultivate—bringing forth food from the earth. . . . There is the sea, vast and spacious, teeming with creatures beyond number. . . . May the glory of the LORD endure forever (Psalm 135:3, 7; 104:14, 25, 31, NIV).

➢ *Takeaway* **Sing praise to his name.**

POWERTHOUGHT Man is a venerating animal. He venerates easily as he purges himself. When they take away from him the gods of his fathers, he looks for others ahead.

—Max Jacob, "Hamlet-ism"

Fifty

FAMILY MATTERS

☐ 344 ______

Blessings on all who reverence and trust the Lord—on all who obey him! . . . Let each generation tell its children what glorious things he does (Psalms 128:1; 145:4).

➢ *Takeaway* **Let each generation tell its children what glorious things God does.**

☐ 345 ______

[Lord], your faithfulness extends to every generation, like the earth you created. . . . Our children too shall serve him, for they shall hear from us about the wonders of the Lord; generations yet unborn shall hear of all the miracles he did for us (Psalms 119:90-91; 22:30-31).

➢ *Takeaway* **Our children shall hear from us about the wonders of the Lord.**

☐ 346 ______________________________

And you must think constantly about these commandments I am giving you today. You must teach them to your children and talk about them when you are at home or out for a walk; at bedtime and the first thing in the morning. Tie them on your finger, wear them on your forehead, and write them on the doorposts of your house (Deuteronomy 6:6-9).

➢ *Takeaway* **Think constantly about these commandments and teach them to your children.**

☐ 347 ______________________________

Let each one of you . . . so love his own wife as himself, and let the wife see that she respects her husband. Children, obey your parents in the LORD. . . . Fathers, do not provoke your children to wrath, but bring them up in the training and admonition of the Lord (Ephesians 5:33; 6:1, 4, NKJV).

➢ *Takeaway* **Let each one of you so love his own wife as himself, and let the wife see that she respects her husband.**

☐ 348 ________________________________

A man leaves his father and mother and is joined to his wife in such a way that the two become one person (Genesis 2:24).

➢ *Takeaway* **A man is joined to his wife, and the two become one person.**

☐ 349 ________________________________

Wives, fit in with your husband's plans. . . . Be beautiful inside, in your hearts, with the lasting charm of a gentle and quiet spirit. . . . You husbands must be careful of your wives, being thoughtful of their needs. . . . Remember that you and your wife are partners in receiving God's blessings, and if you don't treat her as you should, your prayers will not get ready answers. . . . You should be . . . full of sympathy toward each other, loving one another with tender hearts and humble minds (1 Peter 3:1, 4, 7-8).

➢ *Takeaway* **Be full of sympathy toward each other.**

☐ 350 ________________________________

Teach a child to choose the right path, and when he is older, he will remain upon it. . . . The father of a godly man has cause for joy (Proverbs 22:6; 23:24).

➢ *Takeaway* **Let each generation tell its children what glorious things he does.**

POWER THOUGHT Unravel the family and you unravel the warp and woof of society. Your family is wonderfully valuable, no matter what the social theorists say.

Fifty-One

WHEN YOU HAVE TROUBLE FORGIVING

☐ 351

Forgive us our debts, as we also have forgiven our debtors. . . . For if you forgive men when they sin against you, your heavenly Father will also forgive you. But if you do not forgive men their sins, your Father will not forgive your sins (Matthew 6:12, 14-15, NIV).

➢ *Takeaway* **If you forgive men when they sin against you, your heavenly Father will also forgive you.**

☐ 352 ______________________________

Peter came to Jesus and asked, "Lord, if my brother keeps on sinning against me, how many times do I have to forgive him? Seven times?" "No, not seven times," answered Jesus, "but seventy times seven." (Matthew 18:21-22, TEV).

➢ *Takeaway* **Forgive seventy times seven. —Jesus**

☐ 353 ______________________________

Do not stay angry all day. Don't give the Devil a chance. . . . Get rid of all bitterness, passion, and anger. No more shouting or insults, no more hateful feelings of any sort. Instead, be kind and tender-hearted to one another, and forgive one another, as God has forgiven you through Christ (Ephesians 4:26-27, 31-32, TEV).

➢ *Takeaway* **Do not stay angry all day. Don't give the Devil a chance.**

☐ 354 ______________________________

You Lord, are good, and ready to forgive, and abundant in mercy to all those who call upon You. . . . Return to the LORD your God, for He is gracious and merciful, slow to anger, and of great kindness (Psalm 86:5; Joel 2:13, NKJV).

➢ *Takeaway* **You Lord, are good, and ready to forgive.**

☐ 355 ______

There were also two others, criminals, led with Him to be put to death. And when they had come to the place called Calvary, there they crucified Him, and the criminals, one on the right hand and the other on the left. Then Jesus said, "Father, forgive them, for they do not know what they do" (Luke 23:32-34, NKJV).

➢ *Takeaway* **Father, forgive them, for they do not know what they do.**
—Jesus

☐ 356 ______

As the elect of God, holy and beloved, put on tender mercies, kindness, humility, meekness, longsuffering; bearing with one another, and forgiving one another, if anyone has a complaint against another; even as Christ forgave you, so you also must do (Colossians 3:12-13, NKJV).

➢ *Takeaway* **Put on tender mercies.**

☐ 357 ______

If your enemy is hungry, give him bread to eat; and if he is thirsty, give him water to drink; for so you will heap coals of fire on his head, and the LORD will reward you. . . . "Vengeance is Mine, I will repay," says the Lord (Proverbs 25:21-22; Hebrews 10:30, NKJV).

➢ *Takeaway* **"Vengeance is Mine, I will repay," says the Lord.**

POWERTHOUGHT I am forgiven; therefore I forgive.

Fifty-Two

THE BIBLE

☐ 358 ____________________

Happy are those who do not follow the advice of the wicked, or take the path that sinners tread, or sit in the seat of scoffers; but their delight is in the law of the LORD, and on his law they meditate day and night. They are like trees planted by streams of water, which yield their fruit in its season, and their leaves do not wither. In all that they do, they prosper (Psalm 1:1-3, NRSV).

➢ *Takeaway* **Their delight is in the law of the LORD. In all that they do, they prosper.**

☐ 359 ______

The whole Bible was given to us by inspiration from God and is useful to teach us what is true and to make us realize what is wrong in our lives; it straightens us out and helps us do what is right. It is God's way of making us well prepared at every point, fully equipped to do good to everyone (2 Timothy 3:16-17).

➢ *Takeaway* **The whole Bible was given to us by inspiration from God.**

☐ 360 ______

The grass withers, the flower fades, but the word of our God stands forever (Isaiah 40:8, NKJV)

➢ *Takeaway* **The word of our God stands forever.**

☐ 361 ______

Whatever God says to us is full of living power: it is sharper than the sharpest dagger, cutting swift and deep into our innermost thoughts and desires with all their parts, exposing us for what we really are (Hebrews 4:12).

➢ *Takeaway* **Whatever God says to us is full of living power and exposes us for what we really are.**

☐ 362 ___________________________________

Forever, O Lord, your Word stands firm in heaven. . . . Your words are a flashlight to light the path ahead of me and keep me from stumbling. . . . Guide me with your laws so that I will not be overcome by evil. . . . I have thoroughly tested your promises, and that is why I love them so much (Psalm 119:89, 105, 133, 140).

➢ *Takeaway* **Your words are a flashlight to light the path ahead of me and keep me from stumbling.**

☐ 363 ___________________________________

Do for others what you want them to do for you. This is the teaching of the laws of Moses in a nutshell (Matthew 7:12).

➢ *Takeaway* **The laws of Moses in a nutshell: do for others what you want them to do for you.**

☐ 364 ___________________________________

The Lord is our Judge, our Lawgiver. . . . You who know the right from wrong and cherish my laws in your hearts: don't be afraid of people's scorn or their slanderous talk. For the moth shall destroy them like garments; the worm shall eat them like wool; but my justice and mercy shall last forever, and my salvation from generation to generation. . . . I have put my words in your mouth and hidden you safe within my hand (Isaiah 33:22; 51:7-8, 16).

➢ *Takeaway* **The Lord is our Judge, our Lawgiver.**

POWER THOUGHT When in doubt, read the instruction book.

☐ 365 ______________________

As your plan unfolds, even the simple can understand it. No wonder I wait expectantly for each of your commands (Psalm 119:130-131, TLB).

➢ *Takeaway* **Those who wait expectantly for God's direction always find it.**

Other Living Books Best-sellers

101 FUN BIBLE CROSSWORDS. Young and old alike will discover hours of brain-teasing, mind-stretching, vocabulary-building fun in this puzzle-packed collection. All puzzle themes relate to Bible facts, characters, and terms. 07-0976-4

400 CREATIVE WAYS TO SAY I LOVE YOU by Alice Chapin. Perhaps the flame of love has almost died in your marriage, or you have a good marriage that just needs a little spark. Here is a book of creative, practical ideas for the woman who wants to show the man in her life that she cares. 07-0919-5

ANSWERS by Josh McDowell and Don Stewart. In a question-and-answer format, the authors tackle sixty-five of the most-asked questions about the Bible, God, Jesus Christ, miracles, other religions, and Creation. 07-0021-X

THE BELOVED STRANGER by Grace Livingston Hill. Graham came into her life at a desperate time, then vanished. But Sherrill could not forget the handsome stranger who captured her heart. 07-0303-0

BUILDING YOUR SELF-IMAGE by Josh McDowell and Don Stewart. Here are practical answers to help you overcome your fears, anxieties, and lack of self-confidence. Learn how God's higher image of who you are can take root in your heart and mind. 07-1395-8

CHRISTIANITY: THE FAITH THAT MAKES SENSE by Dennis McCallum. Ideal for new teachers and group study, this readable apologetic presents a clear, rational defense for Christianity to those unfamiliar with the Bible and challenges readers to meet Christ personally. 07-0525-4

COME BEFORE WINTER AND SHARE MY HOPE by Charles R. Swindoll. A collection of brief vignettes offering hope and the assurance that adversity and despair are temporary setbacks we can overcome! 07-0477-0

DAWN OF THE MORNING by Grace Livingston Hill. Dawn Rensselaer is a runaway bride, fleeing a man she was tricked into marrying. But is she also running away from love? 07-0530-0

Other Living Books Best-sellers

DR. DOBSON ANSWERS YOUR QUESTIONS by Dr. James Dobson. In this convenient reference book, renowned author Dr. James Dobson addresses heartfelt concerns on many topics, including questions on marital relationships, infant care, child discipline, home management, and others. 07-0580-7

DR. DOBSON ANSWERS YOUR QUESTIONS: MARRIAGE & SEXUALITY by Dr. James Dobson. Practical information about romantic love, conflict in marriage, male and female uniqueness, adult sexuality, and more. 07-1106-8

DR. DOBSON ANSWERS YOUR QUESTIONS: RAISING CHILDREN by Dr. James Dobson. A renowned authority on child-rearing offers his expertise on the spiritual training of children, sex education, discipline, coping with adolescence, and more. 07-1104-1

FOR MEN ONLY edited by J. Allan Petersen. This book deals with topics of concern to every man: the business world, marriage, fathering, spiritual goals, and problems of living as a Christian in a secular world. 07-0892-X

GIVERS, TAKERS, AND OTHER KINDS OF LOVERS by Josh McDowell and Paul Lewis. Bypassing generalities about love and sex, this book answers the basics: Whatever happened to sexual freedom? Do men respond differently than women? Here are straight answers about God's plan for love and sexuality. 07-1031-2

HINDS' FEET ON HIGH PLACES by Hannah Hurnard. A classic allegory of a journey toward faith that has sold more than a million copies! 07-1429-6

JOHN, SON OF THUNDER by Ellen Gunderson Traylor. In this saga of adventure, romance, and discovery, travel with John—the disciple whom Jesus loved—down desert paths, through the courts of the Holy City, and to the foot of the cross as he leaves his luxury as a privileged son of Israel for the bitter hardship of his exile on Patmos. 07-1903-4

LET ME BE A WOMAN by Elisabeth Elliot. This best-selling author combines her observations and experiences in a number of essays on male-female relationships. 07-2162-4

Other Living Books Best-sellers

LIFE IS TREMENDOUS! by Charlie "Tremendous" Jones. Believing that enthusiasm makes the difference, Jones shows how anyone can be happy, involved, relevant, productive, healthy, and secure in the midst of a high-pressure, commercialized society. 07-2184-5

LORD, COULD YOU HURRY A LITTLE? by Ruth Harms Calkin. These prayer-poems from the heart of a godly woman trace the inner workings of the heart, following the rhythms of the day and seasons of the year with expectation and love. 07-3816-0

MORE THAN A CARPENTER by Josh McDowell. A hard-hitting book for people who are skeptical about Jesus' deity, his resurrection, and his claim on their lives. 07-4552-3

MOUNTAINS OF SPICES by Hannah Hurnard. Here is an allegory comparing the nine spices mentioned in the Song of Solomon to the nine fruits of the Spirit. A story of the glory of surrender by the author of *Hinds' Feet on High Places.* 07-4611-2

QUICK TO LISTEN, SLOW TO SPEAK by Robert E. Fisher. Families are shown how to express love to one another by developing better listening skills, finding ways to disagree without arguing, and using constructive criticism. 07-5111-6

THE SEARCH FOR THE TWELVE APOSTLES by William Steuart McBirnie. Through travel, Bible study, and research, McBirnie has uncovered the history of Christ's apostles and their evangelical activities. The dedication and zeal of these men will inspire the faith of every reader. 07-5839-0

THE SECRET OF LOVING by Josh McDowell. McDowell explores the values and qualities that will help both the single and married reader to be the right person for someone else. He offers a fresh perspective for evaluating and improving the reader's love life. 07-5845-5

SINGLE PARENTING by Robert G. Barnes, Jr. Practical, in-depth answers to important questions that single parents have. With biblical insights, Barnes points the way to personal and family healing. 07-5920-6

THE STORY FROM THE BOOK. From Adam to Armageddon, this book captures the full sweep of the Bible's content in abridged, chronological form. Based on *The Book*, the best-selling, popular edition of *The Living Bible.* 07-6677-6

Other Living Books Best-sellers

THE STRONG-WILLED CHILD by Dr. James Dobson. With practical solutions and humorous anecdotes, Dobson shows how to discipline an assertive child without breaking his spirit. Parents will learn to overcome feelings of defeat or frustration by setting boundaries and taking action. 07-5924-9

SUCCESS! THE GLENN BLAND METHOD by Glenn Bland. The author shows how to set goals and make plans that really work. His ingredients of success include spiritual, financial, educational, and recreational balances. 07-6689-X

THROUGH GATES OF SPLENDOR by Elisabeth Elliot. This unforgettable story of five men who braved the Auca Indians has become one of the most famous missionary books of all time. 07-7151-6

WHAT WIVES WISH THEIR HUSBANDS KNEW ABOUT WOMEN by Dr. James Dobson. The best-selling author of *Dare to Discipline* and *The Strong-Willed Child* brings us this vital book that speaks to the unique emotional needs and aspirations of today's woman. An immensely practical, interesting guide. 07-7896-0

WHY YOU ACT THE WAY YOU DO by Tim LaHaye. Discover how your temperament affects your work, emotions, spiritual life, and relationships, and learn how to make improvements. 07-8212-7